William Cowper Prime

Among The Northern Hills

William Cowper Prime

Among The Northern Hills

ISBN/EAN: 9783744651691

Printed in Europe, USA, Canada, Australia, Japan

Cover: Foto ©ninafisch / pixelio.de

More available books at **www.hansebooks.com**

AMONG THE NORTHERN HILLS

BY

W. C. PRIME, LL.D.
AUTHOR OF "ALONG NEW ENGLAND ROADS"
"I GO A-FISHING" ETC.

NEW YORK
HARPER & BROTHERS PUBLISHERS
1895

CONTENTS

CHAPTER	PAGE
I. THE PRIMEVAL FOREST	1
II. A TROUT-STREAM	12
III. AN UP-COUNTRY ARTIST	24
IV. BEYOND	37
V. AN OLD ANGLER	54
VI. DOUGHNUTS AND TOBACCO	67
VII. JOHN LEDYARD	77
VIII. THURSDAY-EVENING MEETING	85
IX. AN EASTER LONG AGO	92
X. AN OLD-TIME CHRISTMAS	102
XI. ALONE AT THANKSGIVING	111
XII. HOW THE OLD LADY BEAT JOHN	122
XIII. PHILISTIS	128
XIV. A NORTHERN SLEIGH-RIDE	135
XV. LIFE SEEN THROUGH A WINDOW	148
XVI. COLORED PEOPLE	156
XVII. EXAMPLE	172
XVIII. THE SIGN OF THE CROSS	180
XIX. A CHILD'S VOICE	191
XX. PURITAN SUNDAY	201

AMONG THE NORTHERN HILLS

I

THE PRIMEVAL FOREST

LONESOME LAKE cabin stands three thousand feet above the sea, in the primeval forest. It is reached by a zigzag bridle-path, cut in the mountain-side, which leads up from the Franconia Notch road. The cabin and lake are a thousand feet above the road. Both road and bridle-path go through the primeval forest. No axe of lumberman has, hitherto, desecrated this forest sanctuary.

The expression "primeval forest" is little understood by many who use it. While there is an almost universal desire to preserve portions of our American forests from the saw-mill, there seems to be everywhere a prevalent notion that this end can be accomplished by a judicious system of forestry, which includes the plan of thinning out the woods, selecting and cutting from year to year some of the older trees, guarding the younger to grow up and grow old, thus preserving and cherishing a perpetual succession of shadowy groves. Well meant though this plan doubtless is, and suited to preserving parks, it would, if carried out, be destructive to the primeval forest, whose grandeur in things large and beauty in things small can only be preserved as they have been created, by letting alone. The forest can take care of itself, but is jealous of interference. It is not a park, nor does it resemble a park. The one is mere nature, the other is art. The natural forest is a world of innumerable creatures, animate and inanimate, who have from time immemorial lived in community. You can never tame the wildness of those people.

Why not call trees people?—since, if you come to live among them year after year, you will learn to know many of them personally, and an attachment will grow up between you and them individually. They will be companionable to you, as are your horses and your dogs, and after a while you will have the same sympathy with them that you have with the next higher order of living beings whom you call animals.

There are hundreds of white-birch trees on the mountain-side, and on the ridge, and around the lake, each of which I know, and of these there are perhaps twenty or thirty with which I have had long relations of friendship. I would not have the woodman's axe touch any tree on this mountain for any money. Every one is a friend. Some, I cannot say why, by reason of one or another peculiarity, are special friends. You would not find it very easy to say what characteristics, differing from those of other persons, make the friends you chiefly love specially dear to you. Nor would it be possible to say why certain trees in this vast forest always seem particularly precious in my eyes; whether it is because of stateliness, or grace, or firmness, or calm strength that speaks of trustworthiness, or because this one looks jovial and tosses his arms more recklessly, or that one is a seemingly sad old fellow, whose forlorn and weary look asks for sympathy.

Often I have questioned one old friend concerning his life story, and he has silently told much of it; wherein is instruction. For the life of a tree has its resemblances to the life of a man, and the latter may find good example in the former.

His youth was passed among difficult surroundings, and the labor of living was arduous. He adopted early the motto of success, whether of a young tree or of a young man, "patience and perseverance." The mountain-side was rocky, and the only soil was the dead dust of his ancestors, clinging among the stones, and mixed with the gravel of decaying granite. At the very start, when he sent out his young roots, they encountered bowlders on every side. Haste and impatience would have ruined him, and left the bowlders masters of the situation. He directed his roots warily around them, feeling along their sides, and drinking rain that dripped from them, and thus the youth grew strong with the help of the obstacles that were in his way. So his full strength was attained, and his roots reached far and interlocked with the roots of his young friends, and they helped one another to stand up in the winds.

All the time there had been one bowlder especially obnoxious and obstructive. But he had been patient, and thrust a root between this and another, greater, which almost touched it. And that root thrived, and though strangely shaped and flattened between the rocks, was healthy, so that when the day of his strength arrived the bowlder was to him no more a trouble; for with the abundant force in that root he quietly shoved the great rock out of his way and forgot it. So patience in the time of weakness prepares for victory in the time of strength.

It is strange that with our changing flesh we bear always the scars of mishaps in childhood. It must be some hundreds of years since a squirrel in midwinter (when squirrels feed on the tender tips of birch branches) ate rather deep, and stopped forever in the sapling the growth of that twig. But just below the end was a branching twig, which the squirrel let alone. Why? I don't know. How should I know what scared a squirrel on this mountain two hundred generations of squirrels ago? The tree's history is recorded, but of the squirrel's nothing can be known except this one incident. How do we know it was a squirrel that bit off the twig? I answer, how can you account for it otherwise? Suggest a better theory, and we will accept it. That's the principle on which half the modern ologies go. Devise a theory and accept it as demonstrated truth, and rest your scientific faith on it, because no one has invented a better theory. I believe in the squirrel, and the evidence that a squirrel bit off that branch is as good as the evidence for nine-tenths of the supposed truths in modern progressive science.

The small ungnawed branch grew out nearly at a right angle to the main stem; and there, when I first knew my old friend, was a huge knee, close to the tree trunk, in one of the branches nearly a foot in diameter, where the twig had started out from the little stem.

I have often wondered what made other scars on the body and arms of my old friend. The stormy life he led I know all about. Who that has wintered and summered in the hill country of New Hampshire does not know it? Every winter was fierce with snow and frost and tempest. Every summer had its stretches of dry times among the rocks and gravel, three thousand feet above the sea, when the white blood ran slow and hot and feverish in the veins. And then came the summer storm, wild, mad, with thunder shaking the mountains, and lightning falling on one and another and another of the trees, sending them down riven and shattered, and then wind, such as winter knows not, heavy wind dragging wet clouds through the tree-tops with awful speed, howling by turns, and by turns hushing down to horrible silence before the next flash of the lightning and the next tremendous gust, wherein all the trees writhe and twist and toss their branches in hopeless struggling. But no —that is only the external manifestation in which the tree, like the strong man, seems at times to give way to the pressure of the trials that environ him. The agony is not hopeless. The strong trunk is not moved. Storms rarely reach the depths of the forest, where the trees, standing together, guard one another. When it is wildest and most fearful up in the tree-tops it is calm below, and the violent gale breathes only gentle breaths of soft, cool air in the depths of the forest. The companionship of the trees in a great forest is a magnificent sight when a storm is raging over them.

There were a dozen of them, near together, around my old friend, of about the same age. Their ancestors had settled here together, among the spruce-trees and balsams. There is a water-course close by them, where in rains a torrent descends the mountain, and where in dry times some water is mostly always flowing down under the rocks and moss and oxalis. Birch-trees love such places, and looking up from the valley you can trace the lines of all the water-courses down the mountain, by the lighter-green foliage of birches contrasting with the dark green of the pines which cover most of the hill country where the axe has not done its devastating work. These old people have grown old together, and it is interesting to see how differently they have grown old, just as men do.

Some were poorer and some were richer. But the wealth and the poverty had no relation to the land they lived on. It resulted from the stuff that was in them, the vigor of constitution, analogous to the will in a man.

There is one mighty old fellow who stands directly on the top of a rock, three or four feet in diameter, and who sent his roots down on three sides of it. So the tree stood on the rock as on a pedestal, and you can see the big stone, hugged by the great roots, under the very centre of the trunk; and he is stout and green and rugged, good, apparently, for a hundred years more. Life and success with him are due to determination and making the most of his small opportunities.

There is another, who stood close by my old

friend, and who is like some old men, shabby in his attire and utterly regardless of his appearance. He had the best of land, and had grown fat on it and lived sumptuously, and when old age came he grew cynical, despised the young modern slips of trees around him, then grew misanthropic and selfish and careless. You never saw such rags as the old wretch wears. They flutter in the wind around his miserable old body from the ground up for forty feet, streamers of bark, some long and black and scarcely holding to him, some rolled up in tight rolls, dingy and dirty. I remember him when he was a noble white-birch, and his dress was snow and gold, and when the afternoon sun shone slanting down the mountain I have seen the fringes of his robes touched with crimson and purple, and his apparel then was altogether royal.

Why did not he go down instead of my kingly old friend? The woods are full of graves of great trees, long green mounds, mossy and beautiful. Why has not that old fellow, who has nothing to live for, lain down to be covered up comfortably, and forgotten?

Many joyous memories are connected with my old friend. Once, years ago, as I came down the mountain, I found on his trunk a scrap of white paper, whereon a friend, strolling up the path thus far, but no farther, had written a few lines from Horace, and another few from Menander, and fastened them there, where he was sure I would find them. Once, years ago, I sat on one of his great roots, and talked with a friend with whom I shall never talk again in the language of this world. Once, years ago, as I came down the zigzag path, I looked across the angle from two hundred feet above, and saw two lovers sitting at his foot, and knew they were telling, with eyes and lips, the old and never-too-old story of young hope. There are lovers in these forests sometimes; for the Profile House is only three miles away, and Lonesome Lake has become one of the sights to see, and it is a charming stroll this way for those who love to wander and talk. They are old married people now, those lovers, but if they came here to-morrow they would not see any change in the forest; for they took no note of trees or rocks or anything, but one of the other. And they would not miss the tree, or know that his is that huge trunk that lies all along the hill-side.

One day I was walking down the path, and, as is my custom, sat down often to look at trees and plants and animals. A northwester was blowing, but this side of the mountain was sheltered, and only now and then a whirl of wind shook the tree-tops. I was looking down the hill-side towards my old friend. A red squirrel was standing on a dead branch, a few feet off, looking doubtingly at me. A woodpecker was at work on a trunk almost within reach of my hand. A white-throat sparrow was pouring out that long, sweet refrain which is most melodious of all forest sounds when heard as the sun is going down.

There was a rustle of the breeze, and a sudden rising of the sound of the river down in the valley, which showed that for the moment the current of air was from the southeastward. And then there was a loud, crashing crack, and after it silence. What internal shock, what violent emotion, what that, to the tree, was like the sudden memory of a great joy or a great grief to an old man, had broken the stout old heart of my friend I cannot tell. Was it that breath of wind? He fell towards it, not away from it.

In the silence that followed the sound of the heart-breaking he seemed to be looking downward for a place to lie. Then slowly his lofty branches glided across among the branches of the other trees, and swept gently downward through them. Two of his companions reached out strong arms to catch and hold him up, but he slipped quietly out of their hold—vain hold now that all was over— and so lay down among the mosses. But he did not lie comfortably with his body on some small bowlder, and he lifted himself up with a convulsive spring, and then lay down again. Nor was he yet at ease. For a moment he turned a little, this way and that way, till he secured his bed of rest, along among the rocks, and then there was perfect quiet.

The south wind stole in softly over him. And the shabby old fellow, who ought to be lying there, fluttered his dirty rags, and seemed to be shaking himself from head to foot with unseemly laughter. Much as I abhor an axe, I am tempted to cut down that old tree. Better—some wet October day I will set fire to his rags, and see the column of flame shoot skyward around him. It will not hurt, only purify him, and he may send out young branches and be a better tree.

No; there is no science of forestry which can preserve the solemnity and beauty of the primeval forest. The one only law to be enforced from generation to generation is, "Let it alone."

II

A TROUT-STREAM

THERE are no streams in all the world more beautiful and grand than are the streams which flow down the ravines of the Franconia Mountains and out into the valleys. It is not to be denied that the State of New Hampshire, by its legislation or neglect of legislation, has reduced the value of the valley lands by destroying the beauty of these streams after they leave the mountain slopes. No one cares to build a country home on the bank of a river flowing with mush of saw-dust, unapproachable except by wading in soft, rotten wood, foul with drifting slab stuff and the waste of sawmills. To see water flowing in all the exhilaration of freedom you must go from the valley to the foot of the mountain, and meet the rivers where they come out from the forest. Or enter the forest high up on the mountain-side and find the spring brook, and follow it down the wild gorge through which it rushes, receiving constantly other streams, and growing into a torrent before it sweeps out on the level country and dies a miserable death, suddenly losing all spirit, vigor, life, and beauty in the mill-dam.

Pond Brook is the name of the stream which, flowing out of Echo Lake on the summit of Franconia Notch, wanders down through a dark ravine some four or five miles, always in primeval forest, until it emerges on the valley lands, and, after a mile of sunshine on fields and farms, is lost in Gale River. There are trout in Pond Brook, mostly small in the ravine, many large in the open country. Times are not now what they once were here. Time was when this brook was one of the finest trout-streams in the world. But times have changed. A large manufacturing village, six miles away, turns out on every Sunday morning in April and May scores of men with poles and lines, who reduce the trout to a comparatively small number. I have counted, on a Sunday morning, thirteen rods following one another within two hours along the bank where the brook meets the river.

Nevertheless, the angler who cares less for the number and size of his fish than for the surrounding joys which make trout-fishing so delightful will not fail to find his reward here, under the lofty slopes of Mount Lafayette, among the fields of Franconia Valley, than which no valley of America or Europe is more beautiful.

There are spots of ideal beauty all along the stream, where I have been accustomed to linger, and forget, and remember. There is one such spot where the river cuts under its left bank for ten or a dozen rods, while the other shore is a broad stretch of gravel. It flows swiftly, three or four feet deep under the high bank, on which various bushes hang in a dense mass of foliage. Then it spreads out over a wider bed of cobble-stones, making as it descends two superb curves of beauty; then takes a straight course down a rushing rapid for ten or fifteen rods more. In this stretch of the stream I have, in the many years that I have fished Pond Brook, taken more trout and larger trout than in any other part of it. It is so open and free from trees and bushes on one shore, that you can use a fly rod with great comfort, and cover seventy or eighty feet with easy casting.

It was warm, though late in the season, when I sat down there, the other day. Golden-rod and asters made the fields bright; once in a while a Vanessa butterfly sailed along, and fluttered his chocolate-black wings with old-gold borders close under my eyes as he paused for a whiff of my cigar. The remains of a barbed-wire fence skirted the top of the bank, an example of the fast prevailing barbarism of the nineteenth century. There is no more barbaric custom in the history of mankind than the use of barbed wire to enclose fields. The express purpose is to hurt cattle. Without the hurting the barbs are useless, and plain wire would do as well. I have seen fine horses ruined by those abominations of modern fencing.

It was a day to sit lazily on the river-bank and look around and think. I took my fly-book from my pocket and hunted through its leaves for some fly which might possibly call up a trout in the rapid. As I turned over the leaves, somewhat listlessly, I found myself thinking of something far away in time and space. It was a very clear memory—or you might call it a vision, seen through the suns and the mists of more than a half-century. I saw another grassy meadow somewhat like this, and a stream not so large as this, winding its way through it.

On the bank, or on a knoll a little way from the bank, sat an old man and a very small boy. The man was a tall, slender man, with a stoop in his shoulders, long arms, long legs, long, thin, gray hair hanging over his checked shirt, blue eyes, a sharp nose, an equally sharp chin. Every minute particular of his dress and appearance came back to me distinctly. The boy was not yet five years old. But, young as he was, he was intensely interested in the instruction he was receiving. The old man was showing him the flies in his fly-book, telling him how he tied them, answering the innumerable questions of the little shaver whom he was teaching to take trout with the fly.

For this man was a renowned angler; and, like all

genuine anglers, was kind to little children, and took great delight in teaching this one the gentle art. At that moment he was explaining that no one ought to tie a fly for trout on anything stouter than a single horse-hair. We had no silk-worm snells and leaders in those days. Nor had we silk lines. His line was made of horse-hair, five or six strands, tapering down to three and two and one. His rod was hickory, two lengths spliced. I do not remember the reel, but from later experiences I think it was a large, wooden, home-made reel. His lessons soon became practical.

The little boy took the rod in both hands, and began casting, or trying to cast. The perverse line behaved as it always behaves with beginners. The old man patiently disentangled it from mullen-tops and tussocks of grass, and with careful fingers extracted the hooks, now from his own shirt and now from the boy's. Once in a while the cast went out well, and the boy with delight obeyed the instructor, drawing, letting the flies go back on the current, drawing across, lifting the bobber and dancing it up on the ripples. And suddenly there was a rush at the tail fly. His little eyes were intently watching the cast, and the rush so startled him that he unconsciously jerked his rod and struck his first trout exactly as he should have struck him.

Then came the struggle. He wanted to lift that fish out with a swing; but the old man held him firmly by his right arm, and compelled him to handle the rod correctly. It was a marvel, has been always since that day a marvel, why that single horse-hair did not break. It held on the gentle spring of the hickory rod while the fish went under one bank and under the other, while he went down stream and the reel paid out and the boy trotted in the deep grass following the trout, and the old man kept firm grasp on the right arm of the little angler.

Yes, he was an angler then, and thereafter through all his life. He killed that trout, a half-pounder—he or the old man, who managed the rod by managing his arm. And when the trout lay on the grass they two sat down again and talked. Many and many a time after that they two sat on the grass by the brook-side and talked. The old man died long ago. But I have in my fly-book a reminder of him—two flies which he tied when he was very old. It was seeing them that brought back this memory as I sat in the sunshine.

While I read my fly-book after this fashion a grasshopper leaped on to the open page. I caught him, and I then caught three or four more, and threw them into the swift stream. They disappeared in the current; but in a moment, sixty feet down stream, I saw a small fish rise and swash the water as he seized two of them in succession.

So I stood up on the high grass-covered bank,

and resumed fishing in fact instead of in fancy. I worked the water thoroughly, beginning with short casts and extending line till I had sixty or seventy feet out. Nothing rose. Then I paid out until the flies (I was using two) were more than a hundred feet away, swinging across and back, in and over the rushing water. I forgot that I was fishing, and watched the action of the flies, practising with them to make their actions life-like, thinking for the moment only that I was dancing flies on a running stream. Then I began to reel in line, and the tail fly flapped in the current close to the bowlders on my shore, while the upper fly, a small golden pheasant feather, hung loosely, swinging in the air three or four inches above the water. There was a trout under those rocks. He had seen those flies for several minutes, and what he had thought about them must be matter of conjecture. Perhaps he suspected them to be shams. Perhaps he was not in a feeding mood. Probably he was in that condition in which men often find themselves, comfortable and lazy, too much so to be easily induced to disturb himself. There are moral lessons to be learned in angling. Here was one. Temptation may be steadily withstood, but the moment of yielding comes like a flash. The price of successful resistance is eternal, unwavering, vigilant self-restraint. Something that was very life-like, a flutter of the wing, a gleam of light on the golden feather, a doubling or outstretching of the hackle legs, a curve in the water through which he was looking—something caught the trout intellect, broke into the caution with which he had surrounded himself, and he went with a rush for that fly.

I, standing on the bank nearly a hundred feet up stream, and knowing nothing of the intellectual struggle going on in a trout's brain down there, was astonished and somewhat startled when a noble fish went into the air, sending a cloud of spray over the fly, and falling with his broad side on the hook. I had expected nothing so large.

Trout take the fly in various ways. They are skilful, by experience. In many instances, when the fly is on or near the water, the fish strikes it with his tail, and turns swiftly to seize it in his mouth. It is a charming sight to watch an insect passing over a shallow where trout are numerous near the mouth of a cold brook or on a broad rapid, and see the tails of the fish dash water at him. Often you may see, as flies light on the water, the broad tail of a large fish swash over one, and then the swirl as the head swings around and the mouth takes in the half-drowned fly. It is very common, therefore, when fishing with flies to hook fish through the tail fin. Often a fish throws his whole body over an insect.

Now and then a skilful trout will leap into the air, mouth open, and engulf a fly in his throat.

This is an interesting sight when it occurs, for you will remember that looking from below the water into the air, unless the view be perpendicular, the line of vision is around a corner, along the angle of refraction of light. The insect is one, two, or more inches away from the straight line of vision, and if the fish leaps for the insect on the direct line of vision he will certainly miss him. Do trout learn by experience the principle of the refraction of light in passing through different mediums?

I did not hook this trout. He hooked himself. As he fell on the fly the hook pierced the skin just below the adipose fin, close to the tail fin. If he had been hooked in the regular way, in his mouth, I should probably have lost him because of what next occurred. The grassy bank on which I was standing was some ten feet above the stream, cut away in the spring freshets so that the turf extended to the edge, and the earth mixed with loose stone sloped steeply down to the rapid, bordered here with round water-worn stones fallen from this crumbling bank. The trout found a moral lesson at the fly end of my tackle concerning temptation. I found another lesson at the other extreme of the tackle, the butt of my rod, "Let him that thinketh he standeth," etc.

As the fish leaped I suddenly stepped forward. The bank gave way like dry dust under my feet, and I sat down with a tremendous thud on the edge of the sod. No, not on it, but in it, for I went down through it first with a crush of earth and dust and stones; then, as my heels dug through the loose material below, with a slow but sure descent which nothing could arrest. I had but one hand to use, for the rod was in my right hand, and that fish was fighting like a tiger on the line, and the reel was paying out, and there was not more than thirty feet of line left on it, and below that rapid was a hole full of brush, whence one could never hope to recover hooks, much less a large trout.

It was a bright day, with a clear sunshine glittering over the rapid. I remember distinctly how my high, black, water-proof boots shone as they descended into the glitter. The round stones continually gave way under me, and I sat down lower, lower, lower in swift progression, until I was sitting up to my waist in the river, my rod by some mysterious instinct transferred from my right to my left hand, while with the former I was bracing myself against a bowlder which was only a few inches under water. But for that bowlder I should have rolled over and over in the current.

Standing up in a stream of water is not so easy as it may seem. Rising to your feet after sitting down in it is wholly another affair from getting up from the ground in the air. Without knowing it we stand, walk, sit up, move about, swing, and manage our bodies by a continual exertion of mind as well as muscle. A dead man cannot stand. A child must learn by experience to walk, and by slow practice acquire the use of the countless muscles, from head and eyes to feet and toes, which are essential to standing, walking, and running. All this experience we acquire in the air. In the water, where a pound of flesh no longer presses downward an avoirdupois pound, much of our atmospheric experience is useless. With a heavy medium like water around us, it is no easy thing to regain foothold once lost. This is why many persons are drowned in water in which, with due presence of mind, they could stand up on hard bottom and walk ashore.

I swung my feet down-stream, and secured a rough hold for my heels. Then I transferred my rod again to the right hand, felt that the fish was on the hook, worked my body into a firm position, gradually found good foothold, and at last stood up in the river. Then I waded across to the shallow gravel bottom on the other side, and began to wonder at the continued vigor of that trout. For I did not know where the hook had pierced him. A trout struck and held by the mouth in a rapid, with his head up-stream, is quickly controlled. The gills, which are the lungs, soon yield to the rush of the water. It was a long time before I got that fish. I don't know how long. He weighed a trifle over three pounds and a half—a fine fish for a mountain stream which a hundred anglers visit every spring.

III

AN UP-COUNTRY ARTIST

THE sun was nearing the horizon. The road ran close by the side of the river. It was a narrow road just there, and the river was but a small stream—a brooklet rather than a brook. But they call it the river, because far down the highland slopes, when it reaches the open country, having received all along its way supplies of water from thousands of springs, it is a river, turning the wheels of great mills, and, farther on, floating ships.

Here it ran between grassy banks, crossing and recrossing the road, which was not even bridged over it. But as we drove on it grew stronger, and when another road joined that on which we were driving another stream came in also, and thereafter the road was better and the stream was larger. Soon the slope which had been gentle on the open upland became more steep. Road and river entered the forest, and plunged downhill together. They never separated for miles, the wagon-track following every bend and angle of the torrent, until, at the foot of the long descent, both together came out on a broad valley.

Three or four miles across the valley we could see the white tower of a church and a mass of elm-trees which hid the village. But we did not go on to the village. For as we left the forest and came out on the plain we parted company with the stream, which wandered away in green meadows, while the road passed in front of a farm-house, standing among sheds and barns, all looking old and weather-worn, but all in good order.

The place had not changed in aspect since I drove up to the door of the old house forty odd years ago. The same stone-walls enclosed the fields, the same clematis vines ran over them, the same white spires of meadow-sweet stood up out of low green thickets, the same choke-cherry trees dangled their bunches of berries above them. The house was equally unchanged. And now, as I pulled up at the steps, the lapse of time was more difficult of realization when I saw an elderly man sitting on the little piazza. For just such a man, without coat or waistcoat or hat, with short gray beard and frizzly gray hair, sat there when I drove away from the house.

Of course, I said to myself, this is not my old host, Eleazar Thorn. He must have gone to the church-yard company years ago. Who can it be?

"They tell me you keep travellers overnight once in a while," I said.

"Yes, we give 'em such as we've got," was the answer; "we don't keep tavern, but when any one comes along that wants to stay with us, why we try to make 'em comfortable."

An hour or two later, sitting on the piazza with my host, whose name I had not yet learned, I asked: "What has become of the Thorn family that used to live here?" He looked at me for a moment as if uncertain what to say; then replied, "The old folks died long sence." "And Ezer?" I asked. Again he looked at me, now a little longer time, and at length said, "I'm Ezer; but I don't remember you."

It is not worth while to relate how I reminded him of the time when, in company with an artist friend, I spent a week at the house, and of the urgent advice then given him to cultivate his evident talent with the pencil.

"Did you give it up entirely?"

"I haven't drawn a picture for more'n forty year."

"Why did you give it up?"

He turned his eyes away from me, let them rove over the country, looked now for an instant at one thing, then looked to another, and at last said: "Well, I don't know as there was any particular reason, only, you see, little Susie died, and there wasn't any one to make pictures for." There was no special emotion in his voice. It was a simple matter of fact in his history which he was relating. But when I remembered the old time, there was in his answer a certain pathos.

One evening, the first evening of our stay, we had come in from a long day's fishing, and, as we approached the house, found Ezer sitting on the piazza step, and by his side a little girl of six years old. He was a large-framed and somewhat uncouth boy or young man. His hands were large, roughened with farm-work, and burned with sunshine. She was a pretty child, with a great lot of curls hanging from a well-shaped head, and a pair of eyes whose beauty I remember through almost a half-century. He was making pictures for her. He had a sheet of brown paper, the wrapper from off some package, and a broad carpenter's pencil. They two were having a jolly time. He was making rapid sketches. When he began one she would lean over, and with her bright eyes follow the broad lines as they went hither and thither over and around one another, until suddenly she would shout, "It's a cow," or "It's a crow," or "It's a fish," and, clapping her hands with delight, exclaim, "Make me another, Ezer."

My companion, older than I, was an artist of fame in those days, and his work is not yet forgotten. You can see his pictures in galleries and read of him in books. He was greatly interested in the sketches made by the boy, and said that he had wonderful ability. He gave him hints, directions, instruction, and when he came away he said, "I shall be surprised if we do not one day hear more of that boy." But we did not. He never left the farm. The motive of the artist in him was only the love of the little one, his sister's child. When the child died the motive was gone forever.

Nevertheless, he was an artist, and a great artist. For, after all, there is but one accurate measure of merit in any work of art—namely, its success in accomplishing the purpose of its production. This principle is not understood as it should be. Whatever other ideas may be held as to the constituents of high art, the fact remains always that if the artist have a purpose in his work and that purpose is not accomplished, he has failed; if it be accomplished, he has achieved success. The major part of criticism is wasted, because of neglect of this fundamental principle.

The domain of art production is immensely wider and more grand than the domain of that which is called criticism. In the arrangement of this world and of mankind in it, the divine order is that art shall supply the wants, minister to the desires, gratify the wishes of men. Nature is God's gift, and art is equally his endowment. That is a very narrow, though it is a very common, belief that the purpose of high art is the product of works which accord with the ideas and please the tastes of a limited number of persons called educated people. The highest education in this world produces only a very little knowledge, and what is called cultivated taste is full of error, egotism, and ignorance. If we ever attain to the superior knowledge of the immortals we shall know how little we knew here, how feeble were our ideas of the beautiful, how rude and rough and graceless were the pictures and statues and poems and other works of our arts which some of us think ourselves able to pronounce immortal. The standards of merit which we shall then apply will not be such as we read about and try to apply here. And this, I think, is very certain: that when we look back at this life and its wants, its desires, and the small measure of supply to them which all our arts and artistic ability have furnished, we shall know that the standards we used were very untrustworthy. We shall see that everywhere have been artists accomplishing as great work, in unknown ways, as those artists whose names are famous. There have indeed been thousands of artists in every country for every one whose name is recorded. There have been Michael Angelos and Titians and Raphaels in almost every hamlet and village of the civilized world.

There was a little girl who died last winter in a farm-house over the mountains. It was a lonesome place, two miles from any other house, and in the deep snows of the winter practically inaccessible. The child suffered greatly for two months, lying on a bed in a small room off the kitchen. On the wall hung a cheap lithograph representing "The Guardian Angel." It was what you would call a wretched mess of color; and when the mother showed it to me, telling the story, I confess that the angel's form and dress were to me suggestive of a cheap theatrical get-up, and the face was without expression. This was its beauty in my estimate.

But there was something in that picture which won the child's heart. In her severest pain she gained fortitude and calm by fixing her eyes on it. Through the nights she waited for morning, to see it when daylight came in at the window. She was sometimes overheard talking to it. To her vision and the soul to which the vision ministers, the angel was one of the messengers of a land where all things are full of light and love and ineffable beauty. The poor lithograph rose in that room to the rank of the Sistine Madonna, or the San Marco saints of Fra Angelico. When she went at last to join other little children in the joy of Paradise she took with her innumerable holy and pure thoughts, a soul refined and much educated for the new life, by the miserable daub, as you and I would have called it, which to her was the perfection of beauty.

And it was as beautiful as any work of art ever

made. Would you dare deny it to the child? Will you argue it with her if you ever meet her? The measure of beauty is in the mind that receives, not in any other mind.

Our own conceptions of beauty change, not only with education, but with conditions of mind. Raphael could not have painted a picture to win that child's admiration away from her lithographed angel in blue and red. Had the child lived she might have grown to admire the Transfiguration in the Vatican, and she might even have grown to admire Turner's blotches of mystery. There is no possibility of foreseeing what, in art production, we may be led to admire and enjoy by the circumstances and associations into which we are led. Nor is there any authority which can tell us what we ought to enjoy. The notion of some writers that there is such an authority, a standard of beauty, is simply a proposal to take away freedom from art purchase and production, and destroy its power.

The world for which that boy Eleazar worked was a small one, but he satisfied all its desires, gratified all its tastes, fulfilled all its imaginations. More no artist ever did. If you say that the great artist has greater thoughts than those of his race and age—a common saying, which sounds in idle words and has in it no intelligible truth—then he too, the farmer boy, had higher thoughts than he expressed with pencil. But of what value to you or to me or to any one are your imaginary "higher thoughts" of the artist if he cannot express them? The world of art is a practical world. To all of us, in every station of life, come, sometimes often, overpowering thoughts, glimpses through mist and gloom of a higher life than we live; conceptions, almost but not quite formed, of greater achievements, nobler works than we are doing. But if we do not realize them, whether we be only commonplace laborers in the ordinary ways of life, or whether we be artists with chisel or pencil, these amount to nothing for the practical work of benefiting or pleasing ourselves or others.

Sometimes it is said that time alone measures the merit of works of art; that those which survive from generation to generation are the great works. This is a false notion. Often the greatest works have perished, having accomplished their purposes; often the inferior have outlasted the changes of human tastes and fancies, and established for themselves the name of greatness. You will find this to be true: that many of those works of art which are most renowned, most talked of, and most written about, produce in reality very little impression on those who look at them now. They are rather curiosities, which must be seen because celebrated, but they produce little effect on the independent mind. This is eminently true of many renowned statues and paintings. Its truth can be seen when the galleries and museums in which these works are preserved are crowded with visitors, and you observe how few linger around these specific works. Nor is it in any degree probable that if you, not knowing their origin, could to-day see works of Zeuxis or Apelles, you would find in them anything to admire.

All this is wandering from the subject, though directly connected with it. Ezer Thorn was a great artist, although he worked for one only admirer, and that one a six-year-old child. All his works perished as soon as executed—all but one. Late that evening, after he had gone to bed, I was sitting in the old kitchen alone, and, having finished reading the book I had brought with me, looked around for something else. Typography was scarce in that old house. My eye fell on a corner cupboard with glass doors, which I opened. In it I found a large Bible.

Whatever estimate you place on this book, my friend, it is a great book for one who wants something to read. It is infinitely the greatest collection of philosophy, poetry, history, law, known to the world of printing.

As I opened this I found on the last fly-leaf a sketch which was doubtless one of the drawings made by the boy artist many years ago. In fact, next morning he confirmed my conjecture, and recalled the time when he made it. Susie had asked him to make a picture of an angel. He had never seen an angel, nor a picture of an angel. He did not know what ideas other people had of angels. So this was an original work. Such works are very rare, very rare indeed. All artists are copyists, in one or another sense. There are certain expressions of thought which have been handed down from age to age, which may be said to constitute the alphabet of art, with which artists write. Angels have been made in pretty much the same way for centuries. They are always very human in appearance. Some of the fifteenth-century artists made them seem more powerful and superhuman by giving them majestic wings; but a later school reduced them to very lovely human forms, with wings which could not possibly lift those forms above the level of earth and earthly things. And mostly angels in art have been nine-tenths human with faint suggestion of the heavenly.

This was a strange picture on the-fly leaf of the old Bible. It was a mysterious whirl as of clouds, but somehow all the clouds, when you had looked at them a while, seemed to be wings, no one independent of another. That which looked as if in the form of a wing was also part of the form of another and another. And there were eyes, not strongly drawn, in fact only to be seen as if by flashes, here and there and everywhere in the whirling cloud of wings. There was no plagiarism here on any other artist. It was a boy's struggle to reduce into visible form his original but vague ideas. It was not a very successful struggle.

It was in vain that I tried to get from the old man some indication of his ideas in that drawing. He had totally forgotten it and why he made it so. Only, he said, that was the last drawing he ever made for little Susie, sitting by her side when she was sick, and when she had asked him for the picture of an angel. He now studied it a long time. Then, oddly enough, he pointed out to me what I had not seen, some lines among the mists, which certainly assumed the form of a child, with garments trailing away into wings.

"Now I remember," he said. "That was Susie; the doctor had told me she was very sick; I was afraid she was going to die. She did die soon after that. I thought of my little girl going away into a strange country alone, and among people she and I didn't know. She couldn't make anything out of my picture. Neither could I. I don't think I ever tried to make a picture after that one. It was such a dead failure." So he, like many other artists, failed because he essayed too much. Possibly Susie might have been satisfied with the picture in former days, but now she was near heaven, and had visions of angels which he had not.

If you and I ever do see angels, what will we think of the pictures of them which we have been accustomed to see here? If we ever see the face of the Virgin Mother, most blessed of women, what will we think of the pictures of her we have here admired—portraits of Roman harlots? If we ever see the combined beauty and majesty of His face, what measure will we accord to the attempts of human art to make portraits of Him?

IV

BEYOND

It was in the midst of a crowded county fair. A man was lying on the ground, surrounded by a hundred others, who could hardly be kept from pushing one another on to the body which lay there, while two doctors were kneeling over it. "What's the matter?" was the universal outcry, and men were pressing in to see they knew not what, but something they supposed to be part of the show. Perhaps it was a pig with two heads, or a calf with six legs, or some other monstrosity. It had happened only a moment before. A drunken fellow had staggered against a horse, and then viciously cursed and kicked the animal. The horse, rightly enough, kicked back, and the man fell. The medical men were together, examining the horses. Both sprang to the fallen man, and the crowd began to gather.

"Poor Joe!" said one of the doctors, at length, looking up and around at the crowd. "Stand back, men—stand back."

The circle widened at once, those behind yielding instantly when the low murmur passed from one to another that Joe Flint had been kicked by a horse and killed.

"Is he dead, doctor?"

"Not dead, but he will be soon."

Standing with the doctors before the occurrence, and standing by them now, was a tall, fine-looking man, the owner of several horses near by. He did not hear what the first one said, for his eyes were on the countenance of the other who knelt by the injured man, with his hand on his pulse and his gaze fixed on the changing face. After a little the doctor looked up and met the eyes of the tall farmer.

"Is he badly hurt, doctor?"

"He's a dead man, Abner."

"Dead!"

"No, not yet, but—"

The man lifted his hat from his head. One and another and another of the men around followed his example, and in a few seconds more than six-score of heads were bared, while silence grew and grew, spreading to the outer circle, and then throughout the grounds. One, two, three minutes might have passed when both the doctors rose, neither saying a word. But all around them knew that the man was dead.

He was a miserable, drunken dog, a nuisance to the community, whose departure from it was gain to all and loss to none. He was a profane wretch, a terror to children on the village street—a man out of whom had long ago gone almost all the characteristics which distinguish man from brute. No one regretted his death. Rather, as the news spread around, each person, man and woman, who heard that Joe Flint had been kicked dead by a horse he had provoked, felt, if it were not uttered by all as it was by some, that "it was a good riddance."

"Abner," said Dr. Gray, as they walked away from the scene, " I want to ask you a question."

"Say on, doctor," said the other.

"Why did you take off your hat when I told you that Joe was not dead yet? If you had waited till he was dead I would have asked no question. It is a common thing for men to uncover in the presence of death. But you did not take off your hat when I said he was a dead man, and you took it off when I said he was still alive."

Abner Whitney was a man of remarkable character in a New England community where were many notable men. A wealthy but a hard-working farmer, he had from boyhood been noted as an extensive reader of books, and yet more noted as a philosophical thinker. His unfailing kindliness of manner, his superior intellectual power, had made him the most influential man in the community. He commanded the respect of all classes of people with whom he came in contact. Once he walked into the great hall of a large hotel, where were gathered men from all parts of the country. He wore his ordinary working-clothes, having come in on an errand concerning a load of hay. Attracted by a free discussion which was going on among the guests, he stopped to listen. One of the talkers, an eminent judge, catching sight of his face and the intelligence of his eye, suddenly appealed to him with "Isn't that so, my friend?" Whereupon he took up the subject and expressed his views vigorously and clearly, in somewhat homely phrase, but with all the more effect on the group. As he was suddenly called away, a young man exclaimed aloud in the old phrase, "Why, he's a gentleman and a scholar."

Yes, he was a gentleman, and his scholarship was of no mean order. He was silent for a little after the doctor's question, and at length said: "The fact is, doctor, I have always very great respect for any one that's dying. It began with me when the minister lost his little boy. You remember. It was twenty years ago." He paused.

"But you don't mean to say you had any feeling of respect for that poor devil, Joe."

"Yes, I mean just that. When that little five-year-old boy died I was just beginning to think a good deal about—about—well, about things in general. I was everlastingly asking myself the reason of things. And the more I thought and read the more I seemed to see that back of all that happens, from the growing of potatoes to the regular rising of the sun, there was some cause that men couldn't find. And when the little fellow was nearing his end, it came across me while I was watching him that he was going behind the curtain I was trying to look through, and would soon know more than I about everything. You can't imagine, doctor, how large that small boy suddenly seemed to me. I can't tell you exactly what I mean by 'large,' but instead of the little one that I had carried about in my arms he was getting to be a giant. No, I hadn't any respect for Joe Flint while he was making a nuisance of himself here, but when you said he was only just alive, and going to die soon, why, I thought to myself how much that fellow was going to know in a little while. Doctor, Joe Flint at this moment is another sort of person than the Joe Flint we knew an hour ago. What he is or where he is, God knows. I don't care to imagine. But while he was here, a man like you and me, and I was looking at him, all the contempt I used to feel for him went away like a flash, and I took off my hat to a soul that was going in five minutes to know more than all the philosophers."

Abner Whitney was a mighty man, of high soul, like the great Hebrew general whose name he bore. And, like him, he did in all things what he believed to be duty, loyal to his God, his country, his principles; and he did it all with a union of firmness and gentleness which gave him great power. The people in a wide district of country not only respected him, but loved him. It is not often that a man wins the love of his fellow-men. Abner Whitney had won it when a young man, and never lost it. It was not only his universal benevolence in acts; but, in addition, the way in which he was benevolent—his manner, his voice, his tone—which commanded the regard of even the rudest and roughest among the people. It was often said of him that no one ever heard him speak harshly or with any appearance of unkindness in his heart, except once.

Was that unkindness? It was a strange occurrence, which lived long in the memories and fireside talks of the people.

Abner and Enoch Whitney were half-brothers, sons of the same father, having different mothers. Enoch was four years older than Abner. From their childhood they had been of diverse character. When they grew up to be school-boys the several traits which marked their dispositions became more and more distinct. All the tendencies of Abner's life were towards the good; all those of Enoch's were towards evil. Enoch was emphatically a bad boy. There was no ill that boys can do which he did not do, from robbing bird's-nests and exploding fire-crackers in frogs' mouths to robbing choice fruit-trees and trampling down beds of choice flowers. Tradition told many stories of the patient affection which Abner showed his elder brother, the efforts he made to shield him from punishments, the unfailing devotion which he displayed in spite of the uniform rebuffs which he met. He never looked for gratitude, and he never got it. Enoch was a rude cub, without a particle of brotherly affection, never grateful, never uttering a word of thanks for kindness; but, on the contrary, ill-treating and abusing his younger brother on all occasions.

The difference of four years in their age was overcome rapidly in their intellectual growth. The younger brother overtook the elder and passed him in school. The two entered college together in the same class, one at fifteen, the other at nineteen. The former was an excellent scholar — a steady, persevering, and acquiring student. The latter was in all respects the reverse, and did not finish the course.

When their father died the young men inherited a property regarded in those days as a respectable fortune. Enoch was a lawyer in the city, Abner having remained at home with his father and mother, cultivating the farm and managing the estate, which included some thousands of acres of timber land.

The will of their father made a just and wise division of his property between the sons, subject to the life interest of the widow, who survived her husband only a few years. Enoch was dissatisfied with the division, and attacked the will, alleging that his father had a weak mind, and that Abner had unduly influenced him. Abner defended his father's memory, and when the will was sustained, and no doubt remained of the wisdom and sanity of the father, offered to Enoch, as a free gift, the division which the latter had professed to think more just. Enoch accepted it, without thanks. Abner's estate prospered. Enoch's vanished in disreputable speculations made in the city. Again and again, when in trouble, Enoch unblushingly applied to his brother for assistance, and never failed to receive the help he asked. Abner kept his secrets, and never spoke of his brother's character or of what he had himself done for him. But there were lawyers and others, town-clerks and county registrars, who knew much of what was going on, and who talked freely. The marvel of the whole country for years was the patience of Abner Whitney with his offending brother.

But few, if any, knew the one chief offence other than the seventy times seven minor offences of that miserable hound, Enoch Whitney. Abner had yielded to him many treasures. The greatest treasure of his life had been, from boyhood up, his love for the minister's daughter. I say his love for her had been the treasure, for he did not possess her love. His brother won that away from him. For years Abner knew that she was secretly betrothed to Enoch, and that Enoch was playing fast and loose with her. Abner made no effort to win her, but he loved her just the same. No one knows the history of this episode in his life further than this: that Enoch won the confidence of the minister, borrowed all his little estate, ruined him, and then ceased to see or write to Mabel. The minister came to Abner at last, as did all that were in trouble, and asked for advice in his old age. Abner knew well all that the minister now told him, for he had eyes, and little that concerned the happiness of Mabel ever escaped his watchfulness. One great fact had escaped it.

Do not imagine that in Abner's treatment of his brother there was any feebleness of mind or manner. It had long ago become well settled between them that the younger brother regarded the elder as an unmitigated scoundrel. Enoch never cheated Abner but once, and after that Abner always recognized the attempted fraud and advanced the required loans, telling his brother very quietly what he recognized. There had been times when Abner conferred benefits on his brother, accompanying them with urgent appeals to his reason, to his conscience, to the memory of their honest father. But he had ceased to do this long ago, as vanity of vanities. Now that the minister had asked his help, he sent for Enoch to come down into the country, and demanded of him an accounting with the minister and his daughter. His power over his brother was ample, and he used it firmly. The revelation which his interposition brought about surprised him. That evening the two brothers walked into the parsonage together, and, while Enoch was silent, Abner deliberately showed the minister the state of his pecuniary affairs, and the arrangement he had made with his brother for their security, and then revealed the fact that Enoch and Mabel had been secretly married a year ago. He did not tell the minister that Enoch had denied the marriage, had laid his plans to repudiate it and destroy all evidence of it.

Some years went by. Enoch had taken his wife to the city. Abner took care to be informed always of the condition of his family. Enoch kept him well enough informed of his own pecuniary condition by applications whenever he was in trouble. Again and again and again the foolish scamp, growing more and more foolish and more scampish as he grew older, attempted to deceive his brother, and seemed to deceive him, and as often the brother seemed to forgive him. Twenty times Abner relieved the actual distress of Mabel and her children on her application. For, ignorant always of Abner's love for her, Mabel never hesitated to apply to the rich brother of her husband for aid; and when she learned the real character of the man she had married, did not scruple to tell his brother what she had discovered. It is much to be feared that Mabel was not worth the love of such a man as Abner. But men of large mental size have often loved women of small intellectual measurement.

One by one the three children of Enoch and Mabel died, and were brought to the country graveyard and buried by their grandfather's side. While she was yet a young woman Mabel became an invalid. The unkind treatment of her husband had much to do with the increase of her illness, and there were dark sayings among the people of the behavior of Enoch in the last few weeks of her wasted and joyless life. She died, and was brought to the family gathering, and Enoch stood by as they closed her grave. Some said he was broken down by grief; but others, wiser, said, as Abner seized his arm and led him staggering away, that Enoch was drunk at the funeral of the wife he had killed. But no one ever heard from Abner one word of ill speech concerning Enoch, nor any suggestion of censure.

But Abner Whitney was human. He had passions like other men. It is small credit to a man or woman to be what is called "good" by nature.

That self-restraint or discipline which suppresses the evil, curbs anger, produces calmness, gentleness, forbearance, kindness, in appearance and in fact, is far more admirable. That this man was exercising strong self-restraint all his life long in his dealings with his brother no one knew. Enoch had been, like many whom you and I know, a business man of reputation in the city, holding his head as high as any, while he was fit only for the jail of the felon. He finally reached his proper place, at a time when a spasm of virtue, seizing on the public, compelled the prosecution and punishment of some robbers. He had more than once forged his brother's signature and been forgiven. But the forgiving brother was powerless to save him now. He went to prison, and died in the course of his first year of convict life. It was said that in his prison life he gave some evidence of repentance. But people did not put much faith in the story.

The country graveyard was on the hill by the church. There was only one tree in it, a giant old-growth pine, under whose shade was much pine trash and little verdure. Elsewhere the ground and the graves were covered with grass, long and yellow in September. The wind shook the grass in yellow waves. It moaned and soughed and sighed through the giant pine. The ground sloped away a little towards the east. It was noticeable, though few notice it in country graveyards, that all the head-stones were at the western ends of the graves, and all the feet of those lying there were towards the east. And for some reason, perhaps the shape and slope of the ground, when you stood on the upper step of the stile coming over the stone-wall, and looked at that enclosure, it struck you at once as somewhat like a group of carriages or boats, and in winter-time always as a group of sleighs, going in close company eastward towards the country from which comes the dawn.

All these had their feet towards Jerusalem, as the custom has been with the Christian dead for many ages. For the pilgrimage is not yet wholly accomplished, although they have laid down here their loads of humanity, and have found rest elsewhere while they wait for the dawn of the eternal day and for the voice of the Leader calling them to take up the humanity again, no longer heavy, because purified, and to go on in labors that do not weary and lives that are perfectly satisfied.

One Sunday morning the minister, not Mabel's father—he was lying outside the church—the new minister, had preached a second-advent sermon. He believed very firmly in the personal return and reign of the Lord in some undated future.

Abner Whitney was much impressed by the sermon, and after the service stood for half an hour in the graveyard with the minister, talking of the subject. It is impossible for any one who believes in the resurrection of the dead to stand in such a place and not picture to himself the scene one day to be visible there. The old man—he was now over seventy—stood near his father's grave and looked along the row of head-stones. The grave of the old minister, Mabel's father, was parallel with that of Abner's father, some ten or twelve feet distant. Mabel had been buried close by her father, between him and her husband's father. There was space left between the two families for Enoch and Abner to lie side by side.

He pondered a long time on that mysterious subject—"What will they look like when they awake? Will the children look like children? Will the old folks have gray hair and pale cheeks? Will Mabel look as she looked at twenty, or will she be the sad-eyed, worn woman we laid here? Will I—will I—what will I look like? What hour of my life has stamped this body for immortal identity? Shall I be the boy of ten, the man of thirty, or old-looking, as I now am? When Mabel and I look at one another again, will she see in my eyes the love of the school-boy and recognize it? Or will she see the truth of that night when I learned that she was Enoch's wife? What will I look like when I, with all the rest of them, wake and go towards Jerusalem above, the mother of us all?" And the thoughtful, perplexed man turned away from the graves and walked homeward, pondering as he walked, until there came into his thoughts the only solution of this puzzling problem, and he exclaimed aloud, "I shall be satisfied with thy likeness when I awake."

The next morning came word that Enoch was dead in prison. Abner went to the distant prison and brought the dead man home to the old house, and ordered all things fit for the funeral and burial. There was then, for two days, in his soul a great conflict. Had he done his duty to his brother always? Had he in truth and in heart forgiven him his countless offences? Could he lay him in the grave and lie down by his side, and when the time for the rising should come could he stand up and say to Enoch and to Mabel, "Come, let us go forward together." To Mabel, yes. To Enoch, no; unless perhaps in prison life there had been some change in that wretched character.

All his life long this man Abner had been given to fierce mental struggles. That outwardly calm life was in reality one of frequent storms, tempests, cyclonic nights preceding serene days. The night before he buried Enoch was such a night.

They stood around, all the people of the country, as Abner followed the hearse into the churchyard and up to the side of the grave. According to custom, there were two bars across the grave, on which the coffin was to be rested before lowering.

Abner looked down into the grave, then up at the blue, and strained his eyes to see through it and beyond. He had seen the side of Mabel's coffin exposed. Stepping back, as they were lifting Enoch's coffin to place it on the rests, with the feet towards the east, he suddenly spoke out, in his deep, stern voice:

"The other way! The feet this way, the head that way!"

He waved his hand swiftly as he spoke, indicating a turning of the body. There was no mistaking his meaning. Men were accustomed to obey him; and, though surprised, they now obeyed him. Probably the minister, alone of all those there, fully appreciated the meaning of the incident. Even to him it was a revelation of the soul of Abner Whitney. As they two left the grave, Abner spoke, more to himself than to the minister:

"My work is done. I have not judged him, and I will not judge him. In the time to come, when we rise, he shall first of all face her and me. I will give him my hand, and he may turn and go with us if God will. But perverse he has been all his life, and his way lay not towards the light. I have put him with his face set in his own way, which was always other than our way. I have done with him. He is in other hands."

Abner Whitney is dead, and they have filled up the space between the grave of Enoch and that of his father. It seems to me utterly impossible for any reasonable mind to form a just and satisfying theory of life which does not include immortality, the resurrection of the dead, heaven and hell.

V

AN OLD ANGLER

THE wind was blowing freshly down the valley, the horses were in good order, and the country was springing up everywhere to greet the late but welcome spring.

My destination was nowhere in particular. A trout-stream ran near the road-side. My horses know a trout-stream well, and are almost sure to stop without a touch on the reins if they see a good place for a cast.

And this was just what they did that morning, though it was something more than a stream and good fishing-ground which arrested them. For on the green grass at the head of a sparkling pool, in a clear, rushing river, a rod or two from the roadside, a boy was kneeling and adjusting a cast of flies. The horses knew what the boy was at, and took it for granted this was the proper place to stop.

"Are there trout in the river?" I asked.

"Oh yes, lots of 'em, but you can't catch 'em very easy; anyhow I can't, but granther can, and I'm learnin' how."

There was a clump of bushes between me and the head of the pool, but as the boy was speaking I saw a line with two flies go out into the air from behind the bushes, and the cast fell on the rip in the pool, and as it came up towards the foam there was a swash and dash of the water, and the line straightened out taut, and then cut the surface as it swung across towards us. As yet no rod or fisherman was visible, but in a few moments both emerged to view.

An old man, wading in the shallow edge of the stream, stepping with caution, but firmly, came into view, his eye fixed steadily on the pool, and as full of light and brightness as a boy's eye. He knew what he was about, that was plain enough. He did not look up for some time, but when his glance caught the horses and buckboard, and met mine, he nodded cheerily, but quietly held to his work. It is quite as pleasant to see a fish handsomely taken as to take one yourself. He held his rod in the right hand, well up, and the bend away down to the butt spoke of a weighty fish. The first few rushes had been controlled before the angler came in sight, and now the trout was hanging low down in the water, and swinging slowly from side to side of the pool. Passing his rod to the left hand, he began to use the reel, with judgment, and the fish came nearer. Then he rushed, and the fingers left the reel to run, and the rod bowed a little down to the stream to ease the strain, and I saw his finger press on the line against the rod below the reel to make it drag more heavily. So the fish did not go into the swift water below the pool, but, yielding to the persuasion of the rod, turned and gave it up.

In less than five minutes he lay on the green grass, and I weighed him—a plump three pounds; and then I looked up to meet the smiling face of the old angler.

"The boy says he is learning to take trout. I fancy he couldn't have a better teacher."

"Well, I ought to know how to take them here. I've fished this river every spring nigh on to seventy years."

"You began it young."

"Not so very young. I'm eighty-one, and I've caught trout since I was seven years old."

"And like it as well as ever?"

He looked first at me, then at the river, then up into the sky, and swept a glance around the scene before he replied. Then he said, with emphasis: "Yes, just the same as ever. When I had hold of that trout I was thinking of a four-pounder I took out of this pool when I wasn't fifteen years old, and I felt just as I felt then. I don't believe it's in human nature to change one bit in feeling about taking trout from ten years old to a hundred."

There was a keen pleasure in talking with an experienced angler of this sort, and we talked as cheerily as anglers love to talk. He told me a great many things worth remembering about the habits of the fish in that river. For the habits of trout, like those of men, are different in different localities. Hence it is that books of instruction, and rules about flies for certain seasons, and written ways of fishing are of small account. My experienced friend took no stock in the imitation theory. "Sometimes," he said, "but not often in this water, a trout takes a fly because it looks like a fly of the season; but mostly, I think, they are tempted by the variety which is offered them in something alive and eatable which they haven't tasted before. A trout is a greedy eater. In the freshets he crowds his stomach with sticks and stones and everything which goes along in the thick water."

"Are trout of this size plentiful here?"

"No, no. The river is well stocked; but of late years the average size will not be much above a quarter pound. But every spring I get three or four fish running from two to three pounds, and a few pounders. There's another in the pool as large as this one. I saw them both rise a while ago. Will you try a cast?" And he offered me his rod.

"No, I will not interfere with your sport."

"Not a bit of it. I would like to see another man take that fellow better than to take him myself."

"You belong to the true brotherhood," I said; "but I will use my own rod."

"Try this one. I made it myself last winter, a year ago, and it will serve you well."

It was a capital rod, made of the wood of the tree commonly known as shad-blow or sugar-plum. He told me he had trained and straightened growing trees for years before cutting them. The rod was in two pieces, spliced and wound, and weighed perhaps ten ounces. The line was of horse-hair, a marvel of braiding, without an end out anywhere to catch in the guide-rings; and the flies a black tail-fly and a golden hackle bobber. I looked at him as I looked at them, and he answered my look. "Yes, they are all home-made."

Surely it would have gladdened the soul of Izaak to meet this lover of the gentle art. For after I had cast in vain over the pool and wasted my energies for naught, as he sent his flies down under the overhanging bank, where I had been with mine a dozen times, up came that other trout to the golden hackle, and, taking it, was taken.

We passed the day together along the banks of the stream, going for an hour to his home near by for dinner, and coming out afterwards to talk rather than fish by the side of the water. My friend was a very gentle old man. How could one be otherwise who had been for seventy years a lover of the most refining of all arts! The valley in which he lived was very familiar to him, but familiarity had bred love, not contempt. He had never desired to live elsewhere. His life had been passed among scenes that were full of beauty, and their beauty had entered into and become part of his soul. He had no very extensive knowledge of books, but the few books he did know he knew well, and they were books worth knowing. Wise as men may grow, the wisest, after all, know but very little more than their fellows. And this calm life had given to him much knowledge which renowned philosophers have not, and could not have, but by just such experience and education as his.

Before the sun had set we were seated on the veranda of his house, and he was telling of his early life in it, with his wife, long gone.

As, in after-years, I learned more about the character of the old farmer and angler, I learned that he was very fond of living over again that long past, in which his house had been well filled with a large family. Now they had mostly scattered—some to the city, one to the Far West, two to the farther away country. These two were mother and daughter. And though it was more than forty years ago that they two went away, Isaac never ceased to be fond of talking about them, and always talked of them only as "gone away." To hear him you would have supposed that they went away only a few days ago. The lapse of time had been to him as nothing since his wife and eldest daughter left him in the house with two sons, and nothing of womankind to be cared for or to care for him.

He talked this evening of his wife, for something I said reminded him of something which she once said. A trifle was always enough to set him to thinking aloud of either his wife or child—Bessie the mother or Bessie the daughter.

"Come along with me," he said, "and I'll show you what I call their portraits." And he led me a little way from the house through a grove, down a short, steep path, into a ravine—a very wild and very beautiful spot, especially at this moment. For it opened out to the westward, and the light that follows after sunset was pouring up between the overhanging trees and struggling against the brawling stream.

A little way up the brook was a high, large rock, much moss-covered, in the front of which was a curved hollow, forming a sort of rude niche or recess. There was a bench, ancient and decayed, made of a log, hewn flat on the top and supported on stones. Three persons could have been comfortably seated on it. Overhead, on the top of the rock, were masses of fern, and groups of fern-moss were hanging on the side of the slope, making an exquisite drapery. The rocks in front of the bench were white and shining. For when the brook was high it overflowed them. Altogether this was as beautiful a spot as you could well imagine.

"There they are," said he, sitting down on a stone and fixing his eyes on the niche. "There they sit, just as they used to sit. What would I care for a painted picture of them two, when I can see them any day, sitting and working and talking."

"But I can't see them," I said, "and you can't make your friends know them."

"And it ain't important I should. They don't belong to you or to any one else. There's 'Siah Stevens, he lost his wife ten years ago, and he's got a painted picture of her. It was made for him by a first-rate man, too. They say he's a great artist. He used to board at 'Siah's in the summers. I never saw him painting. They said he didn't paint trees and mountains and such things, like most of them that come here. But he painted 'Siah's wife for him, and 'Siah shows it to everybody; and 'Siah's got another wife, and they have new boarders now, and she shows the picture to them when they first come, and she says: 'That's 'Siah's first wife, and she was painted by the great Mr. ——, who used to board with us.' Us! Yes, she'd say *us!* But what's the good of that picture to 'Siah, I'd like to know. Sometimes, perhaps, when she was expecting company and had fixed herself up, and set herself to look genteel, maybe she looked like it. But most o' the time Judith didn't look a bit like that. All the portraits I ever saw have the folks dressed up. Perhaps in cities the women-folk do keep all the time looking that way, and maybe their husbands and children remember them mostly in such dress, and it's right to get them painted so. But I should think a man would get tired of seeing his wife all the time in one colored dress, with her hair slicked, and the same fixings on her neck. No, I don't want any painted picture of Bessie for myself, and no one else has any real care to know how she looked. If they ask you, you can tell 'em. And it's a great deal more important, then, to tell them how she looked to me than how she looked to strangers."

I did not ask him, but he saw in my eyes the question; and after a moment's silence he went on talking, in a somewhat low and dreamy voice. I will not attempt to write his words, but, oddly enough, it struck me at first, not oddly at all as it seemed on reflection, his description of his wife was more an account of the impressions left on his mind by her mind than any description of her person. Unconscious poet that Issac was, like Byron's, his similes were of thoughts, not things. She was beautiful to him, he said, as beautiful as this very evening. And she was just as gentle and quiet in her ways as that streak of rosy cloud in the glow of sunset. She wasn't a softly, no-action girl or woman. She had a mind, and when she cared to show it she was knowing enough. But no one ever heard her speak a harsh word to man or boy or beast. "What color was her hair?—well, it was the color of those pine-trees on the mountain this afternoon." Now, my good friend, do not imagine that pine-trees on a mountain-side are green. There's no green about them sometimes, and when the evening sunlight is slanting over them they are often, as then, a golden brown.

"Her eyes? They were dark, dark as—dark as—dark as—well, they were dark as it is in the night sometimes when I'm lying awake thinking of her."

"It has been a lonesome life for you."

"No; not a bit so. I'm lonesome once in a while, but somehow I never yet seemed to get to thinking of her gone. Mostly it's with me as it used to be in the evenings when she was sitting on the other side of the table sewing, and the children had gone to bed, and I was tired o' the day's work, and we didn't talk much—mayhap never said a word the whole evening. But we were just as contented to keep still, and I'm just as content to keep still now and see her as I can all the time. You know it's a kind of selfish love for your friends that can't be happy except when you have them around you. I'm certain sure that she's happy, and I don't doubt she likes me to be happy, and I think she sees me much of the time just as I see her—I mean she sees into me. I know I think more of what she was than what she looked; and that's the way I suppose she thinks of me now. These are pretty hard-looking hands," and he held up his brown, hard hands; "but I don't think she notices their color or much worries that they ain't as shapely as they were when I first knew her. But whatever they find to do I think the good Lord lets her know it's done as it was when she was here, honestly always, and I expect that's a comfort to her. You see, when you come to have some one that's very close to you gone over to the other country, and you've put their body in the graveyard, why, a sensible man gets to thinking more of himself as something else than his body. Otherwise, how can he think about them that's gone and keep on talking to them?"

"But, Isaac, they don't answer when we talk. That's the hardest part of it."

"Now I ain't so sure of that. You see, the body's over there. She hasn't got any lips to speak words with, and you can't expect to hear what you used to hear. But it's just like this, according to my mind: When I was particularly glad, or particularly sorrowful and troubled about anything, many a time I'd sit and talk for an hour at a time at Bessie, and she'd listen and never say a loud word. But she'd answer, and say her say, all the same. I'd look at her, and she'd look sorry, or kind o' smile, or her eyes would bright up, and all the time I was talking she'd be answering every word, and giving me her opinion, and what she thought I ought to do and how I ought to feel; and it did me a great deal more good than if she'd talked it all out. Now I expect I get just the same kind of advice and comfort from her. Anyway, I tell her everything everyday, just as I used to."

"You have discovered one of the great joys of life, my old friend," I said. "They who are gone away are doubtless waiting. For the end is not yet, and they, as also we, are still looking forward to another life, into which none will enter until all go together, in the body. Meantime, how much they know of us, and how much they say to us, in the voiceless language of the intellect, the universal language which all men of all times and nations, living here, or gone away, understand and use— how often they are the suggesters of our thoughts, the guides of our decisions, the promoters of our happiness, we cannot measure. They make the saddest error in life who bury their dead, body and soul, out of sight and out of reach, and consider them as sent away to wander alone until the resurrection among the countless ghosts of all the human race who have gone before. You have the true secret of happy lonesomeness, for you keep your dear ones around you, dear now as ever."

"Why shouldn't I? It's better and happier for

them, too. Just suppose Bessie coming here to see and talk to me, and finding I wouldn't see her, wouldn't hear her, had set my mind that she was gone, and that was the end of it. Would it suit her?"

Happy are they who live conscious that life is surrounded by an innumerable cloud of witnesses. Happy, too, they who have the beloved so close to them in their hearts and lives that they need no painted portraits to recall faces which would otherwise be forgotten.

I accepted his invitation, and spent the night with him. In the morning, as I took the reins to drive off, the boy stood by, looking somewhat as if he would like to go away too and see the world. "Good-bye, my boy," I said. "Don't go away from here; there's nothing in all the world worth leaving this spot to see; grow up like your grandfather, to be a fisherman and a man." I consider the advice sound. I hope the boy will take it.

VI

DOUGHNUTS AND TOBACCO

HAVE a cigar, or a pipe? Do you know much about art in pipes? There lies open a great field for an art book. Shapes and kinds of pipes have been described, but the art ornamentation of the great peace promoter must be in infinite variety and abounding beauty if one can judge from a few specimens. Look at that Persian sheeshee, with its elaborate arabesques in black enamel. Was there ever a more perfect gem than that Dresden pipe-bowl, painted with the myth of Cupid and Psyche? Or that Berlin porcelain head of a fish, colored from nature?

Coffee, tea, tobacco, the three luxuries which have delighted and enlightened mankind, have all three evoked the highest talent of artists, probably because they are alike luxuries which make men and women contemplative, receptive, ready to appreciate and calm to enjoy whatever is beautiful. The Turk drinks his coffee from an exquisite fingan, held by a zerf, on which Saracen art exhausts its richness. The Chinaman takes his tea from an egg-shell cup of wonderful fineness, blazoned with symbols of peace, home loves, good wishes, in enamels rivalling sapphires and rubies and emeralds. The North American Indian, however little he knows of sculpture, carves his red pipe-bowl into some shape to please his eye, while the civilized smoker employs sculpture and painting to decorate his enjoyment.

There are some men afflicted with the idea that these luxuries ought to be eradicated; who worry themselves to death and write newspaper articles because people drink tea and coffee and smoke tobacco. I don't know whether any of the anti tea and coffee men are left alive, but some anti-tobacco men still contrive to sustain existence.

No anti-tobacco man has yet invented a reason against smoking which is not equally strong against ice-cream, water-ices, iced-water, apple-pie, or doughnuts.

The doughnut is a good subject of comparison. The prevalence of doughnut eating in the interior of New York and northern New England is appalling. Medical science which does not agree about tobacco is generally down on doughnuts. And doughnuts in the morning! Think of them. In northern New England few breakfast-tables have been set for fifty years, public or private, without doughnuts. If up-country gravestones told truth you would find ten saying "died of doughnuts" where one said "died of tobacco."

The anti-tobacconist is fond of appealing to the statements of unknown medical men who have said tobacco is unhealthy. He knows perfectly well that for every one such there are two or ten medical men who deny that it is unhealthy. Medical science is that only on which doctors agree. The weight of medical opinion, backed by the practice of medical men, is in favor of smoking. We are not talking about excessive use of tobacco. Cold water in excess is poison. Milk in excess is deadly. All medical men agree that doughnuts are dangerous.

"It is an expensive luxury." Yes, according to the tobacco you smoke. What if it is? That is no reason why a man who has the money to spend should not spend it for tobacco, or doughnuts, or fine clothing, or beautiful and pleasant things. The argument may apply to the man who spends more than he ought, but is nonsense when carried to the extreme that all expense for luxuries is wrong. The men who use this argument against tobacco exhibit its fallacy in their own persons, clothed in luxuries where rough, undyed garments would answer all their needs. It is one of the notions of communism, which is unable to see the stagnation of equality in property. The arts of beauty, of making objects of luxury, are the support of modern civilizations. Repress expenditures to buying mere necessities of life, and one factory of cotton goods would supply the wants now supplied by ten; ninety per cent. of the labor would be thrown out of employ; commerce would cease; governments would perish.

The duty of the man who has money to spend it on reasonable luxuries is beyond question, unless we agree to reduce life to barbaric conditions, forbid all the refinements and adornments of civilization, live in huts, clothe ourselves in skins and undyed woollen stuffs in winter, and dispense with all clothing in August. No, we can't accept any argument that our expenditures must be reduced to the bare necessities of life. We were made, by a good maker, with powers of enjoyment. Taste, smell, sight, hearing, touch, all are given, not only as means of life, but as means of receiving pleasure, gratification, delight. To be happy in the use of the senses is God's blessed gift to humanity. Some enjoy pie, cake, doughnuts; some enjoy tobacco. The expense is no argument against the man who, having the money wherewith to buy doughnuts or tobacco as he prefers, or both if he likes both, buys and smokes tobacco.

But the anti-tobacco man says it makes a bad odor. He omits to say that it is bad to his nose. There is no greater impertinence than this of making your nose the governing nose in society. It is probable that a large majority of noses in America, Europe, Asia, and Africa, and in each country taken separately, regard the odor of tobacco as very agreeable. But that is nothing to the argument.

It only proves that odor is a matter of individual taste. If the odor is disagreeable to you, that is a first-rate argument that you should keep your nose out of the way of tobacco smoke. It is also a good argument against smoking in public places. But it is no argument against smoking at Lonesome Lake Cabin. You think it an evil that away up on the mountain, three thousand feet high, in the free winds, I smoke tobacco. Confine your attention to this point. It is a good way to get at the abstract question of the right or wrong of smoking tobacco. You will observe that all nasal considerations here are to be determined by my nose and not yours, and your argument on odor is not applicable.

Do I hear you say that it is a bad odor, and I ought to dislike it? Pardon me, but that is a common sort of impertinence. Nothing is more ridiculous than to insist on our tastes as good, and other people's, which differ from ours, as bad. Your nose in not to be poked into other people's business. Probably you have always thought no one has a right to go into society with perfumes disagreeable to you, and that you have a perfect right to use musk or violet or geranium or anything that you think people ought to like. It is a great blunder. Your nose is for your guidance and gratification, not for mine. That is God's law, given with human senses.

The odor of tobacco is not only pleasant to me,

and pleasant to pretty much every one of the visitors to the cabin, but it is pleasant to the most lovely inhabitants of the world around. If on any sunny afternoon of summer you visit us among the mountains you may see a sight to do your heart good. When we sit in the soft air on the piazza smoking quietly, there are gorgeous butterflies, such as Cupid might well love, which scent the aroma from afar, and come hovering around, and light on our beards and mustaches. As the twilight falls over us, great sphinx-moths, rich in color and swift of wing, poise themselves in the air close to our faces, and breathe the odor which they love.

But you say "tobacco stupefies the intellect and senses." Nonsense, man. Don't talk absurdities. It makes dull intellects brilliant, and gives brilliant intellects new vigor. It rests the weary, refreshes the worn, consoles the depressed. For every profound thinker since the seventeenth century, every great teacher, poet, philosopher, preacher, every man who has benefited the human race by his intellectual labor, for every one of these whom you can name as not a smoker of tobacco, you yourself know two or four or ten who smoked. Your argument is so thoroughly and stupidly untrue that it never could have been uttered by one whose intellect did not need the awakening influence of tobacco.

Perhaps you say "smoking leads to drinking." I

have heard anti-tobacco men say so. This is another absurdity, without a shadow of truth. Smoking allays thirst. Doughnuts lead to drinking. You can't eat two without taking a drink, and if there is any cider around you will be tempted. If there is no cider you will be drinking beer or whiskey or something bad for you. No one can drink cold water with doughnuts. They don't go together in reason. This argument is good against doughnuts, but not worth a cent against tobacco.

"But some men who smoke also drink." Yes, and some who smoke work, and study, and visit the poor, and are charitable and useful, and pray. Try the argument on that proposition and see what it is worth.

After all, do you drop back on the last resort of the one who has no sensible argument and tries abuse? You say that Dr. Somebody said a cigar was a thing with a fire at one end and a fool at the other. The only possible answer to such an argument is in kind, and there can be no reasonable doubt, if he did say it, that Dr. Somebody was a donkey, whether his name be Aristotle or Franklin.

And now, having exhausted argument and abuse, you ask me why I smoke. You want a reason in favor of smoking. I could give you a hundred, but one is all sufficient. I like it. I like good doughnuts and I like good tobacco. That is conclusive and binding on you until you show it to be wrong.

I like it. The scent of burning Latakia is sweeter to me than sickly roses or effeminate odors of violet. In the perfumed cloud are many visions. Why, man, it grew on Lebanon. Jebel-es-Sheik, Hermon of old, the sheik of mountains, looked from afar down the hill-slopes of Laodicea. Every evening refreshed the young plants with dews. The sun that rose in the morning from beyond Damascus and Palmyra and Nineveh shone on Jerusalem while it ripened them. The soil from which they rose is dust of Egyptian soldiers of Sesostris, flying Persians from the field of Issus, and pursuing Macedonians. When the smoke rises from it, you can see wonderful shapes and shades that go floating among the rafters of my cabin, crowding one another, till, unless you have gotten used to them, you will begin to think of going out into the less uncanny and more familiar society of the woods and stars. You don't know what treasures are packed for thoughtful smokers in every bale of that tobacco. Each bunch of those leaves, in which history, imagination, and enjoyment are condensed as in few printed leaves, was chosen carefully by a son of Ishmael, and mingled, as he knew his friend's taste, with the Koranee, which gives life and force to the shapes and shadows born of the burning Latakia. He has sent me many small bales of those leaves, and from time to time I have given them away or burned them to call up the spirits. They remind me, too, of him, and of the many times in years past that he and I have slept in the cool night air falling from Hermon, or looked down in the morning from that hill-side at the blue beauty of Galilee. Till the next bale comes, if ever it come (for alas! long silence bids me fear my friend is dead), that little remnant in the gazelle-skin bag is reserved for evenings of happy memories.

It is no light business, when a man is growing old with his pipe for a companion, to hurl at him a lot of your inanities about his bad habits. You, who do it, must be well assured that you are in sound mind and senses before you enter his house with your notions, your ideas of right and wrong, your nasal perceptions and affections. If you prefer in crowded rail-cars and public places to breathe hot, feverish breath, foul with the smell of all kinds of food and with diseases from all sorts of lungs, possibly others may prefer the breath purified by smoking some herb. In many countries where smoking is allowed in some and prohibited in other public carriages, nine-tenths of travellers, ladies as well as gentlemen, prefer to ride where smoking is allowed. Be sensible, then, and don't subject yourself to a reasonable charge that you are a mere public nuisance yourself with your constant iteration of your personal dislikes, and your everlasting projecting of your nose into public notice. Contend as much as you please that men and women who use perfumes, who eat garlic, who perspire in hot work, who smoke tobacco, or who otherwise make themselves perceptible to other people's noses should stay at home and not annoy those noses. That has nothing to do with the propriety of smoking tobacco in quiet homes like Lonesome Lake Cabin.

It is so complete a puzzle to know what it is which worries the soul of the man who writes savage abuse of tobacco, that we, who would gladly relieve him, are unable to afford him any consolation.

Come up to the cabin this summer, and learn to smoke. The first may, but I don't believe the second pipe will make you sick in this mountain atmosphere. And you will be a better man for it. You will feel better yourself, and take a more kindly view of the world, and of people whose noses are built on principles differing from yours. If you want to argue the question we will argue it. Only, before you come, go carefully over your prejudices against smoking, and see if your reasons do not apply with much the same force to doughnuts.

I will not join you in an argument against doughnuts. One must have some respect to his reputation in New England.

VII

JOHN LEDYARD

As you come up the Connecticut Valley to the mountain country you have without doubt often noticed the quiet beauty of the river under the forest-covered hill at the station of Hanover and Norwich. Hanover, with Dartmouth College, lies a half-mile or so from the station, on the New Hampshire side, concealed from the rail by the high land and trees on the eastern bank.

Often as I pass on the rail or drive through Hanover and across the bridge to White River village I never fail to recall, in imagination, a scene on the river-side a hundred years ago, when a life of wandering may be said to have begun which thereafter led all over the world, and had sad and solemn ending on the bank of the Nile, within sight of the pyramid of Shoofou.

When I was a boy the name of John Ledyard was more familiar to boys and men than now. Perhaps it was more familiar to me because he was a family relative, and my father had letters and memorials of him, at which I looked sometimes with wondering interest.

Dartmouth College had been in existence but two or three years when the Hartford boy was sent there to be in some sort under the direct charge of President Wheelock, a friend of the family. I call Ledyard a Hartford boy because, although born at Groton, he had been taken in hand by a relative, Thomas Seymour, of Hartford, and had been at school and commenced reading law in the Connecticut city. It was a small city then, and part of Ledyard's boyhood was passed in Mr. Seymour's house, which stood somewhere on the bank of Little River, now called Park River; then doubtless a clear stream.

He was about twenty years old when his restless disposition made it evident that the law was not his vocation. He never could obey, and restraint of any kind was to him intolerable. Oddly enough he took to the notion of becoming a missionary. I suspect from the circumstances that he had vague ideas of the charm of life among the heathen and small concern about their souls. Dartmouth was in wild regions. Indian boys were students there. The idea of becoming a missionary among the savages was attractive. The very life at the college in the northern wilderness presented tempting features. So with a horse and two-wheeled carriage he started, carrying his baggage and sundry possessions, for the long drive from Hartford to Hanover. There was no road, except here and there from one to another settlement. But he went safely through. It is a notable fact that this would-be missionary to the Indians carried with him the rude outfit of a theatre, scenery and curtains, wherewith to amuse himself and his college companions, white and copper colored. And it seems too that he established theatrical performances at Hanover, and I am not aware that Dr. Wheelock interfered to interrupt their successful run.

A year or so at Hanover was all the restless boy could stand. Once during that year he had disappeared for some months, and it is supposed had in that time roved among the Indians, perhaps, as far as Canada. The experience probaby dispelled the romance of missionary life, which had thus far inthralled his imagination. His horse and sulky were gone. History does not record their fate. He was far away from civilization. But daily he saw the strong flow of the Connecticut downward towards the distant sea, and across the sea lay the islands and countries of the great world, and many unknown countries full, in his fancy, of marvellous adventures.

Close to the bank of the river he felled a great forest tree, whose vast trunk gave him a log fifty feet long and three feet in diameter. This he fashioned into a boat—not a canoe, as is sometimes written, but evidently a dugout. His college companions helped him, probably Indian boys as well as white boys. Did they know his purpose? I fancy not. They were the pioneers of college boating-clubs; and as you whirl along the iron track to-day you can with fancy eye-glasses see across the river, under the overhanging trees, that group of jolly boys, working with fire and steel, burning and hewing, chatting and chattering, full of life and vigor and fun, while the vast log takes shape from day to day. They are all dead long ago. I have no catalogue of the Dartmouth alumni, and know nothing of any of them. Whatever their lives thereafter, they were all more or less characterized by wondrous adventure. There never was a human life which had not in it passages of the sort we call romance—passages of deep emotion, strong conflict, great pain or great joy. They are all dust now, those boys, and from the living flesh and bone and sinew that worked on Ledyard's boat at Dartmouth in 1772 trees have grown large and strong—birches and maples here, palm-trees in Africa.

The boat was finished, and in a starry night of April, when the river was running full with the melting snows of the mountain country, the young voyager stole down to the shore, pushed off into the current, and began his wanderings.

He made choice of companionship which, incongruous as it may seem, was not strange when we consider his character. He had provisioned his boat, and took his bear-skin for covering. For company he carried his Greek Testament and his Ovid, and drifting down the glorious river, than which none on earth runs through more beautiful and varied scenery, he lay rolled in his shaggy covering and read now the wildest romances of Greek and Roman mythology, now the eternal truths of revelation.

Of his adventurous voyage we know nothing except that as he approached the 'gorge at Bellows Falls he was so intent on one or the other of his books that he barely escaped being drawn into the rapids and hurled to destruction. But he escaped, dragged his dugout around the falls, and resumed the voyage. So it happened that Mr. Seymour and his family in Hartford were surprised one sunny morning at seeing this strange craft coming from the Connecticut up the Little River, stopping in front of the house and discharging a solitary voyager, the once intended Indian missionary.

Thereafter followed fifteen or sixteen years of roving life, realizing in the main all the imaginations of the boy. With Captain Cook he went around the world. Alone he penetrated the depths of Siberia. He was always travelling, travelling, travelling.

It is not probable that at any time in all his fancies and forethinkings had ever come to him any imagination of the end, and least of all of such an end as he at last reached. In Cairo, whither he had gone with intent to cross Africa to the western sea, and where he had concluded, after three months of anxious delay, an arrangement with an Arab merchant to take him a thousand miles and leave him then to force his own way to Timbuctoo, just at the moment of packing his luggage for the start, a sudden illness and a fatal overdose of medicine arrested his wanderings on earth, and the restless boy of Dartmouth, the reckless voyager on the Connecticut, went suddenly, without scrip or purse, to see the wonders of the undiscovered country.

No one knows where he was buried. Elsewhere I have written of my vain attempts in Egypt in 1855 to ascertain something about this. I renewed the inquiries a few years ago in Cairo. But the search was utterly hopeless. Even the Moslem lets his father's tomb crumble without repair, and an Eastern cemetery is always a ruined graveyard. But he was, of course, not buried in Mohammedan ground. Neither is it certain that Greek or Copt or Armenian or Latin would admit his poor dust to the companionship of their dust. It was a curious, a very remarkable search which I made, in all and every of the various monasteries and churches in Cairo, Fostat, and Boulak, seeking some trace of Ledyard's death or burial. I had long interviews with very aged clergymen, longer interviews with custodians of pretended records, which proved to be no records, and after all I was left to the longest interviews with my own imaginations, in the wonderful glamour of Egyptian evening lights, when the sun was going or had gone down into the Libyan Desert.

Many times every year I pass along the riverbank at Hanover, and see that group of boys under the trees hewing out the boat. Many times I have come up the river-side in the night, and have seen the solitary voyager drifting down the current under this same old sky. And so it occurs that while other travellers see only the beautiful river and the dark trees which still shade it from the forenoon sun, or perhaps the glitter of moon or stars in the ripples, I see more. For, unlike the boy who fancied far off a golden sunlight on a free and roving life, I see a straightened form, made for strength, but very still; a face of exceeding beauty, but now set and calm; surrounding people wearing strange robes, uttering no words of sorrow; a grave in the yellow sand, where the desert meets the Nile flood; the sun gone down, the twilight coming over the pyramids and flooding around the Mokattam hills, in haste to claim the valley for silence and gloom, the flood of the Nile flowing to meet the flood of the Connecticut in the one great sea, and the Hartford boy at rest, alone. But not alone. For the rivers of human life that have flowed in many ages through many valleys, like the rivers of Asia and Africa and America, have poured their counted and numbered drops into one great sea. And when Menes and Osirtasen and Thothmes come crowding back with the sons of Israel and Ishmael and the men of Phœnicia and Macedonia and Ethiopia, to seek in Egyptian dust their own dust, wherewith to be reclothed, the pale face of the Hartford boy will shine in the new light, and he will find the ashes which I vainly searched for.

VIII

THURSDAY-EVENING MEETING

It was unusual for me to make such a blunder. I had forgotten the road directions given me five miles back, in the last of the twilight, and now it was dark—very dark—pitch dark. I was alone in my buckboard. It was blowing a gale, and the rain was driving in wet blankets. I was in haste, for the road was yet long before me, and the speed we had kept up till darkness came was still kept up. I could trust the horses reasonably well to turn out if they met anything, and as to driving, it was just no driving, but only sitting with reins in hand and letting things go.

I did not see the school-house till I had come alongside of it. It stood at the fork of the road, and we had taken the right hand. As I caught sight of the little windows through which dim light shone out I knew that I was passing the school-house, where I had been told to take— Which was it—the right or the left? I pulled suddenly on the reins and the horses slowed. The next instant I thought I remembered that I was to take the right-hand road, and on we went. Although at the instant I was not conscious that I had heard anything, yet for a second or two, as I went away, sounds from the school-house came faintly to my ears, and there was enough in them to assure me that I had heard, before I thought of it, the singing of a hymn by several voices. The tune was familiar. The words were, "Who are these in bright array, this innumerable throng?" and then I was passing under a large tree, and the wind and the branches were making a sound which was like the roar of a cataract.

In ten seconds I knew I was on the wrong road. The words of my direction came back suddenly and distinctly: "Left hand at the school-house, right hand fifty rods beyond it." So I pulled up and inspected the position. You can turn a buckboard short around by getting out, taking the hind axle in your hand to lift the hind wheels around one way while with your other hand you turn horses and fore axle around the other way. This I did, and when it was done I lighted the lantern which hung over the front of the dash-board.

Back we went to the school-house. And this time I listened. All was silent as I came near, then suddenly the voices broke out again with indescribable richness and melody:

> "Hunger, thirst, disease unknown,
> On immortal fruits they feed."

You say I thought it musical and melodious because of the contrast with the howling storm in which I was driving. Possibly so. I don't know that that makes any difference in the fact. In all the arts, the correct test of the power—the merit—of the work is its effect on the individual whose opinion is concerned.

As I turned slowly around the front of the little school-house I saw, standing in the porch, a boy of fifteen or thereabouts. "What's going on here?" I asked him.

"Parson's a-preachin'; Thursday-evenin' meetin'," he said.

"Hold the reins; they won't move. Stand still, boys," I said to him and to the horses, and pushed open the door.

There were just fifteen persons in the small room—five women, five men, five boys and girls. There were four candles lighted, two on the unpainted wooden desk of the teacher, two at the rear of the room, each in a tin candlestick on a scholar's desk. One of the men was in the chair at the teacher's end of the room. He was an old man with white hair. His face was one of much interest, and I would have been tempted to study its lines but for the fact that a light seemed to shine out of it which compelled notice. They were all singing, he with them, and the hymn ended as I stood in the doorway.

There was music, melody, sublimity in that hymn sung in that little school-house by those people. Time was when the character of New England was full of the influence of such meetings as that, held in scattered school-houses all over the country. The student of American history will make grievous error who shall omit from his considerations the power of the Church exerted through the weekly meetings as well as the Sunday services. They were largely prayer-meetings. This one was a prayer-meeting, and when, after a half-minute of silence, the man with the white hair began to pray, I fell on my knees in front of the door. People in the up-country of New England are not used to seeing men kneel when they pray. Only two girls and a boy saw me. The rest sat with their backs towards me, and dropped their heads forward. It was too late to change my position, nor was it necessary. I had knelt under the impulse of the voice, which was the soul of humble entreaty. The words with which he began, "We beseech thee," were as heaven-reaching in their tone as any response of choir or voice you ever heard in the litany. The prayer was brief, and every sentence in it was a compact petition, for I think every one could be found in Holy Writ. Before the people had raised their heads I had quietly come out, resumed the reins, and went plunging along the dark road in the tempest.

But dark as it was, I was no longer alone. An innumerable company of thoughts, if not of persons, attended me. The voices of the stormy night were not, as before, confused sounds of nature unrestrained. They became, and this without imagination, intelligible utterances of that Omnipotence which governs the natural as well as the invisible world.

For in this life of ours, wherein the employments, the pleasures, the annoyances, the troubles, the griefs, the desires, and the successes or failures of men occupy all our attention and thought, there is nothing which so completely lifts a man out of his apparent surroundings into view of his real surroundings as prayer. Not necessarily his own prayer, but the sight, the sound of some one else praying.

When men are sick and send for the minister, nothing which he can say to the sick man has any such power over the mind as what he says when he speaks to another world and the God who, he believes, hears him. If you see and hear a person talking to another who is invisible to you, you do not doubt the existence of that other, unless the speaker is insane. So, when men hear the sound of prayer to God they have a strong conviction that the speaker is speaking to some one he knows, some one who hears him. And I am inclined to think that among the influences with which the character of New England was moulded in former years, none was more powerful than the prayer which boys and girls as they grew up were accustomed to hear, Sundays and week-days, addressed to the invisible God.

They grew up with a consciousness of subjection to an authority higher than any which they made by voting at town-meeting. That sense of subjection made better citizens than ever can be made without it. It is essential to a good and wise governor or master that he know how to obey, how to serve. The man who is conscious, or even who has only a vague idea of the existence of a power absolute over him and over his State and his country, is a restrained man. And he is a happier, a more comfortable man. There is tremendous power and great satisfaction to the honest man in the knowledge that in the midst of his good and evil, pleasant and unpleasant surroundings, he can speak and be heard in a world very far away from this, and be heard by a willing hearer.

Whatever you think about it, my friend, I think that the best part of the American character, the strength, the trustworthiness, the good blood of the body politic was in the prevalent consciousness of responsibility to God. There is not so much of it as there once was. The blood is thinner than it used to be in some parts of the body, and other parts show symptoms of blood poison.

As I drove on through forests which scarcely made the night seem any darker, now along the banks of wild torrents, now across flats where the water lay deep over the road, I thought much as I have here written. And constantly would come to me the sound of that grand hymn, with its glorious vision of the throne and the white-robed hosts around it. And I thought of that little company, doubting much whether you can find anywhere fifteen persons gathered in any assembly more of whom are worthy or likely to wear those robes.

IX

AN EASTER LONG AGO

THE village road ran due north and south. It was very broad, full a hundred and fifty feet, with large old trees on both sides, standing in not very straight line on the outer edge of the sidewalks. These trees were elms and maples, mostly, which had been planted by former generations. Among them stood an occasional horse-chestnut, later introductions. The elms were mighty trees, some of them gigantic, spreading their arms and hanging their long branches down over the wagon-road on one side and over the sidewalk and the front yards, and sometimes over the houses, on the other side. The houses were continuous, one yard adjoining another, on each side of the road (street, they called it there) for a quarter of a mile from the river bridge at one end to the cross-road corners at the other end of the village. At the cross-road stood the two churches, on corners diagonally opposite one another, and on the alternate corners the village store—the only store—and the village tavern.

The Episcopal church stood in the graveyard, which stretched along up the road. The Presbyterian church had no graveyard. The village was a very old one; the two churches were about equally old. For much more than a century the people of the village and of the rich farming country around it had been accustomed to worship according to the manners of their fathers—some in one, some in the other church. For the most part there had never been any religious controversy or any tendency to it among them while they lived, and when they died they all lay down peacefully side by side without controversy in the village burial-ground.

There came a time when controversy arose. It came, as it often comes, from a cantankerous Christian of one or the other church, who made himself offensive to a member of the other church, and thus began a quarrel. It was of no account at first. But as months and years went on the people—first the women, then the men—began to be ranged on the two sides of the dispute. What it was about no one now knows, and it is not altogether certain that in those days any one knew. Enough that it produced a very wide breach in the social constitution of the neighborhood, which lasted for many years.

The ablest and most influential man in the community was Silas Lawton, a lawyer, a man of wealth for the times, an elder in the Presbyterian church, about fifty years old, living in a fine old house next door to the tavern. He was a gentleman by birth and habit of life, given to extensive reading, and the last man in the world to take part in a village quarrel of any kind. But none of us are free from the influences of our surroundings, and Mr. Lawton had persuaded himself that the most important question of the day for that neighborhood was whether the door of the Episcopal church was not the gate of hell. He probably came to a conclusion finally when he heard that his professional rival and personal friend Thompson, a church-warden of the Episcopal church, had said that he would as soon enter a heathen temple as a Presbyterian church.

Here were two ordinarily sensible men, men of intelligence, behaving like two fools. And for that matter, on this subject all the community were fools —all except the two clergymen, who respected one another, recognized one another as earnest servants of one Master, and were accustomed to hold familiar intercourse.

Something which the Episcopal clergyman had always done in his church, lighting some candles, or putting water into the communion wine, or wearing a peculiar dress—in short, some particular part of the ritual—had become a subject of talk, then of severe animadversion, among the people of the other church. And Silas Lawton had spoken very strongly on the subject, and had then gone further and condemned everything in and about the Episcopal church. In particular, he furnished to the village newspaper articles, not apparently controversial, on Church history, in which he demonstrated to his own satisfaction that the Church calendar is all wrong, that Christmas is months out of the way, that Good Friday is not the anniversary of the Crucifixion, and that Easter is by no possibility the correct date of the Resurrection. In short, he made havoc of the whole business of Church anniversaries and celebrations, and rejoiced some people while he angered others. Thus religious animosities were raging in the village when a series of events happened.

It was in March—a cold, tempestuous March. Old Dr. Malen, the dependence of the people for forty years, died suddenly. Next day Silas Lawton's only child, Fanny, the best-loved, brightest, best-worth-loving girl of fourteen ever known, was taken sick. The nearest medical man lived twelve miles away. They sent for him, but he was off on a distant visit, and word was left for him to come. But he did not come, and Fanny was very, very ill. All that night the wind made moans in the leafless elm-trees, and the soul of Silas Lawton was in anguish. The morning brought no relief. There was plenty of sympathy, plenty of help from neighbors; but help that did no good, for no one knew what was the matter with the girl. Why did not the doctor come? It was not till another messenger had been sent and returned that they knew the reason. He too was sick. No help could be expected there.

Late in the afternoon a travelling-carriage drove up to the tavern door, and three persons sought lodging for the night. Their appearance produced a village sensation. Not a dozen of the people had ever before seen a Sister of any religious order. A horror of Roman Catholics characterized many such villages as this. It was soon reported that three "nuns" were at the tavern, and their journey, whither and wherefore they were going, formed the subject of talk in every house that night.

It came to the knowledge of these ladies by merest accident that there was great distress and anxiety in the house next to the tavern. They inquired the particulars, and the landlady told them all. The eldest of the three is described in the village traditions as of impressive appearance, speaking in a low voice which commanded attention by its suppressed music, looking with eyes that gave one the idea they had no desire to see anything on earth — patient, calm, long-suffering eyes which expressed no emotion, unless patience be emotion. She sent the landlady to Silas Lawton to say that a lady, a stranger, who had some knowledge of disease and medicine, proffered her help, if perchance she could be of any use.

In brief time Fanny Lawton was in the best of hands. She was dangerously ill. Some say it was a case of lung-fever, inflammation of the lungs, or pneumonia in one of its forms. Others say it was a quick fever. Others have other theories. Those three Sisters fought the enemy all night. In the morning two of them went on with their carriage, but the eldest remained. It was a Thursday morning. That day the opinions of people were somewhat divided as to the course of Silas Lawton. Some thought he did well enough. Others thought he had taken a fearful risk in admitting this nun into his house, and especially to the side of his dying daughter. Why, she might baptize her secretly, and so make a Romanist of her; or she might make the sign of the cross over her, and so do her some awful harm. Who could tell what evil might be done by such an emissary of Satan? By Friday the opinions took definite shape, and Mr. Lawton was severely censured.

He cared nothing and knew nothing of this village talk. His life was very much bound up in that child. His love for her was abounding, controlling. He had always known that he loved her, but he never knew a thousandth part how much. Therefore, time, village talk, all were unheeded, and his whole soul was intent on the fluctuating signs of life or of death in that room. Powerless to do anything himself, he could only look on. But much he looked into the patient face of the unwearying nurse, much he sought some expression, some promise, out of those calm eyes, but in vain. Somehow, for a long time, when she was kneeling by the side of the bed, it never came into his head what she was doing, and doing so often. Then suddenly, when it flashed into his mind that she was praying, he fell on his knees. And when the landlady, who saw it, told of this outside, people said it was incredible that Silas Lawton should be seen kneeling and praying with a Roman Catholic.

Friday and Saturday went by. It was late on Saturday night when the Sister told him that she believed the child would live. Still they watched by her all night.

Again the wind was up, now a gale from the south, and the sounds, although perhaps to other ears the same, were to him wholly different. For now he had hope. He had more than hope. He had somehow confidence in that stranger, who seemed to him sent from God. The voices of nature, which he had always heard, as most men hear them in accord with their mental conditions at the moment, now seemed to teach him new truths. In reality it was only that his own reasonable soul was teaching them, because for the first time in his life he was in a receptive state.

Before daybreak the Sister told him she was sure that danger was past, and added that she had been so confident of it the evening before that she had arranged at the tavern for horses to take her on. He was startled, and at first tried to keep her. But no, she must go; and he could not but think she had done more than enough for him. He tried to thank her, but she said, simply, let us thank Him, and turned her face to the east, where were the signs of the dawn. Making a sign on her breast, she bowed her head. He did not make the sign, but bowed his head as well.

Then over him came tumultuously a hundred thoughts—how in old times Christians had prayed, looking eastward, because thence comes the light of the world breaking on its darkness; because thereaway are Jerusalem, and Calvary, and the Olive mountain whence He ascended; because, because—what mattered it to him the reason now? —God had given him back his child through the faith and work of this woman, and he would thank God, looking eastward, westward, anyway-ward, now, and forever hereafter.

And she went, leaving him happy but dazed. The sun was rising as she drove away. He saw it rise, and his eyes were tremulous or the air was tremulous or something intervened, for the sun danced, actually danced, in the hazy air which followed the southerly rain of the night. He looked down the road, eastward, whither the stranger had driven. He went in, and Fanny's eyes greeted him with a look that went to his heart.

"Where is she, father?" she whispered.

"Gone away," he whispered back.

"Where to?"

"I don't know."

"I know," she said; "there's a Catholic church and a convent at W——, and it's only thirty miles, and she will be there by church-time."

"Why by church-time?"

"Why, father, it's Easter Sunday."

Then he went out again and looked up the road, down which the sun was shining. Now he remembered about the sun dancing on Easter mornings, and the memory did not offend him. Now he began to say to himself that he was in very close sympathy with every one who served the same Lord. He began to think—I cannot write what he thought, but this was what he did: He went into his little conservatory and cut every flower there, and made a splendid bouquet, and took it across the street and put it on the communion-table in front of the pulpit in the Presbyterian church.

It was the first time he had ever offered a flower to God. When he had done it, it seemed to him wonderful that he had never done it before. And when, coming out, he met the minister and told him what he had done, the minister was glad, for he had wanted some such help as he was now assured of. And they two judiciously guided things so that the people yielded their prejudices, and great peace followed in the community. The strongest influence was that which came from the Sister. No one knew her name. She had only said she was Sister something—a Latin name they had not remembered. They began to think she was a good servant of her Master. And herein she had done His service in a way she did not know. Some time, in a country where there are no misunderstandings, some of those people will meet her. Many have already met her and know her by a new name, and all of them will understand one another, measuring each other by their likeness to Him.

X

AN OLD-TIME CHRISTMAS

It was a great while ago. That expression conveys various ideas of lapse of time. It may imply only a few months. To a child of ten it might mean five years. To you it may suggest ten thousand, a thousand, five hundred, a hundred, or fewer years. There is a country in which they do not measure time, as we do, by tiny watches or rolling worlds. I am thinking about that country to-night, as pretty much all of us do think more or less about it at this time of year.

A library in one way illustrates the prophecy of the angel that "Time shall be no longer." Around me, as I write, covering all the walls from floor to ceiling, are books. Some are the everlasting, the imperishable thoughts and words of souls who, thousands of years ago, counted time as we count it, and who for thousands of years have ceased to count it. Others are of later ages, of men and women who lived and wrote when the sun and the planets and the stars stood in relations to one another quite different from those they now occupy; of all the successive ages, from the old Chaldean whose thinkings are cut in cuneiform on the seals which are reproduced in various modern volumes, down to the Christmas story writer of A.D. 1890. And all the books, the undying thoughts of people of dead and buried generations, stand solemnly together, all thoroughly alive and wide awake, intelligent and intelligible, living, speaking beings. The material things of the world measure time, and are worn and wasted by time; the spiritual, the thoughts of men, remain immutable and powerful. The companionships of the immortals are not like our companionships who now know personally only the few who collide with us in this short life. Have not some of those, whose thoughts embodied in books are thus brought together in my library, also met one another?

Is there anything strange or improbable in the idea that two or three people, wholly unlike, may have met elsewhere, even by some such accident as caused the meeting of their thoughts on yonder shelf? It happened in a simple way. I had been referring to several authors, and their books lay in a pile. A child came into the library with a book in hand, which she had found in another part of the house. She read awhile and left the book lying on the old theologians, and so all the books happened to go up on the shelves together. Therefore I laughed a little when I saw the old picture-book, the *History of Puss in Boots*, a thin book, squeezed tight between Thomas Aquinas on Job and Augustine *De Civitate Dei*.

I don't know and I don't care who wrote *Puss in Boots*, though his thoughts do seem for the present as imperishable as those of the Philosophers of the Greeks and the Fathers of the Church. But on the fly-leaf of that book are, in manuscript, four words between two names; the first the name of a boy, and the last that of her who gave the book to the boy "a long time ago." And the four words, embalming the thought of one who wrote them, are as eloquent as any words of philosophy or theology —are words which in theology express the infinite difference between the Christian religion and every other religion. For in no other system does the idea appear, which is the foundation idea in the Christian faith, that the God who made and governs is related to the man who neglects and forgets and rebels against him by the relationship of love. "With the love of"—those are the words between the two names. They were written on a Christmas Day a long time ago.

There are several men and women, elderly people now, who remember the young beauty of "Cousin Sarah" and her matronly beauty when she lived a centre of happiness and beneficence. On that Christmas Day, a long time ago, there were gathered in the old house a large company, mostly children, who had come up from the city to spend Christmas week with grandfather and grandmother, hale old people.

Sarah was the eldest of all the grandchildren, a woman grown, for she was twenty years old then, and she was the only one who had been brought up by the old people and still lived in the old home. All the others were much younger—from fifteen down to five. She was, in fact, hostess, and a capital one they thought her then. There had been the jolliest sort of a morning when the stockings were opened, and the customary tempest of young delight, which made the large house ring as it never rang but once a year with that purest of cheery music, the voices of happy children.

All the morning Sarah had given herself to the innumerable cares of the household as well as to the fun of the children. Then to the door came the big sleigh, into which grandpa and grandma were stowed on the back seat, and as many small folks as possible piled in; and behind it came up Sarah's horses and cutter. You would have stood a long time in a colder day than that (the thermometer was ten below zero in the early morning) to look at that beautiful structure, the cutter, itself snow-white, with here and there a touch of gold. But you would have stood longer to look at the horses, magnificent blacks, with human eyes, full of gentleness and fire combined. And you would have looked with all your eyes had you seen that equipage when it rushed off in the brilliant sunshine, she holding the reins, a boy of six years old on either side of her in the cutter, only their small faces visible above the piles of white fox fur that filled the cutter.

The church was three miles away, in a scattered little village. Service was not over till half-past twelve. Then, as she was taking the reins in her hands, the village doctor came up with a quick step.

"I am sorry to tell you, Miss Sarah, that Tommy Grove is not doing well to-day. The fact is, I'm afraid, in our Christmas occupations, we have let him be forgotten, and—"

"I *have* forgotten him. Thank you, doctor. I've neglected the boy, and to say I have been very busy is no excuse."

"I— Really, Miss Sarah, I didn't—"

"Yes, you did, doctor, and you did right, and I thank you heartily. It's not too late."

Away went the horses—not towards home. A half-mile down the road they stopped before a small, shabby house, with a broken gate blocked open in a snow-drift, through or over which a narrow trodden path led to the door.

"Come in with me, boys. It will do you good."

The interior would make a sorrowful Christmas picture. A bare room, with a little poor furniture, a good fire on a hearth where bricks were scarce, a round griddle hanging from a crane over the fire, a pan of buckwheat batter on the floor, two cakes on the griddle, a stout woman in the middle of the room, and a sick boy in bed in the corner, scarcely to be seen through the smoke of the fat from the griddle which filled the room.

The boy's little thin features lighted with a smile when he saw his visitor, and fell again when she told him she had only come to see him for a moment. But he brightened again when she said she would come again before night. A few questions to him and to his mother, some cheery words, and all were out again in the cutter and flying over the country. It was seven miles to the town, where were the court-house and several stores. The black horses knew the road, and knew that their mistress was in a hurry. The sleigh-bells did not jingle or ring, but just swung out a sharp, shrill, tremulous cry of bronze, which cut the air like a knife as they swept townward.

One mile from town there was something strange in sight ahead. You could see it a half-mile away. It was a drunken man, fallen over, out of the track, on the two-feet-deep snow, and lying as if dead. She pulled up by his side. The boys were afraid. Not she. She calmed them, got the drunken fellow on his feet close by the cutter, then tumbled him over into it. If he had been a stranger, doubtless she would have done the same, but this was no stranger. He was the son of her grandfather's old friend, long dead. He had been a brilliant man, educated and respected, now a vagabond. He lay still enough after she saw that his head was all right.

The horses stopped in front of the principal store. A dozen ready hands relieved her of the miserable load, and relieved the two boys of the terror which had possessed their small souls for the last few minutes. In the store the scene was not as it would be to-day in such a store. The world had not then a thousandth part of the things for Christmas merry-making that we now have. Toys for children were few and simple. Books were scarce and expensive. While she was making her purchases one of the boys discovered that book, *Puss in Boots*, and the two together were enraptured with the dauby pictures, colored by hand, wherein is shown how the bright cat enriched the marquis, her master.

"Come, boys, it is time to be off."

"Oh, Cousin Sarah, do look at this book; it's so funny."

"I'm in a great hurry. Bring the book with you, if you want it, Johnny." And back we went, like the wind, over the white road, and through the white land. Then, indeed, the boys thought nothing of that whiteness, nor did it enter their young heads that they were riding with Cousin Sarah in a holier light than that of sun on snow. The swift horses were not more heedless than they of the radiant company of angels who, in after-years when they recalled that sleigh-ride they knew must have accompanied them. The land, the fields, the hills, the road-side, all were white. But as that splendid vision flashed along the road the horses' feet filled all the air around them and behind them with dust of gold, as of the streets of the celestial city.

Again they were in the room where the sick boy was wearying away the lonesome Christmas afternoon. In a moment, with tacks and hammer, parts of her purchase, she transformed the room into a gallery of art of wonderful beauty. Beauty, I say, for beauty is never in the object, but always in the eyes that look and see. Right well she knew that law—sensible, beautiful Cousin Sarah; and she had sought and found beauty—not for herself, but for Tommy Grove. Children had not in those days the wonderful works of art which are now abundant. But she had selected from such as we then had. Tommy lay silent with open eyes, opening wider and wider, filling all the time fuller and fuller of joy while one and another and another were put up where he could see them easily. There were pink children playing, and blue children praying, young ones in sacred and profane history and story, and conspicuous among them all there was a somewhat rude, but to him how lovely, picture of a Mother, in blue robe and yellow kerchief, holding in her arms a Child. It was the Christmas centre, centre of all beauty, now and forever.

"Where have you been with these children, Sarah?" asked the grandmother, as they came into the old house; and the grandfather looked the same question, both of them at the same moment looking also their entire love and trust. And when she said, "Grandpa, I had forgotten Tommy Grove," they looked at each other and said nothing. That evening she wrote in the *Puss in Boots* book the name of a six-year old boy "with the love of Cousin Sarah." And the book is not out of place between St. Thomas and St. Augustine.

I am not that boy. A long time ago he died. Not so long time ago Cousin Sarah died. While she lived her life was a benediction to many young boys and girls, and to many others, old and young. There are some such people—not many—whose whole lives are, like that Christmas sleigh-ride, in the dust of celestial gold, in the sunshine of the better country, with continual attendance of angels. Only her thought, a loving thought for the boy, remains here in her handwriting. She now knows such saints as Elizabeth of Hungary; and they, and such as they, are gathering roses in Paradise.

XI

ALONE AT THANKSGIVING

THE house stood near the road a half-mile or less from the church and store and tavern, which might be called the centre of the village. It was not much of a village; only a dozen or so of houses seattered along the old country road. They were all old houses, and stood under old trees. For this was one of those villages, not uncommon, wherein life had been very much the same for several generations, and that which we call progressive civilization had not invaded it. Even when a railway was constructed through the valley running parallel with the road, and a station was established fifty rods from the church, no one had been tempted to build a new house, no increase was produced in the value of land, no mill or factory was erected on the bank of the stream.

This house was the largest and best in the neighborhood. It was of the kind now called "colonial"; a large two-story double frame-house, with a front door in the middle opening out on a porch a little wider than the door, and opening in to a broad hall which separated the two large rooms on the left from two like rooms on the right. It had an extension, an L in the rear, for the kitchen, and behind the kitchen a good-sized dairy-room, and beyond this a wood-shed, and beyond the wood-shed the stable and carriage-house, and beyond that the barns. Very sensible, roomy, comfortable houses are those old "colonial" houses. In the north country they were cool in summer and warm in winter, and when heavy snow-storms came the entire establishment, from front parlor to barn, was accessible to man or woman without going out-of-doors. There was one great fault in this plan, a plan which prevails still in the building of modern farm-houses in northern New England. That fault consists in the danger from fire. When a fire occurs in such a house in the country, where fire-engines are unknown, if it once gets beyond control it sweeps everything in one conflagration. I have seen a fire starting in the barn work its destroying way to wood-house, dairy, and so on through the whole establishment, while a hundred men stood around powerless to arrest it.

This old house was well kept up. Looking at it you would say that its owner was well-to-do. He was more. He was very rich. He had from youth up retained possession of the homestead, and all that was in it, and had lived there. Much of his time had been passed in the city, but he had no house there, and this was his home. Its ancient furniture was rich, and he had added to it abundant stores of luxury for the delight of the eye and the body. He was no miser. He valued money, rightly enough, only for its purchasing power. But he had never for an instant conceived the idea of using that power to purchase any gratification for any one but himself. Whatever he wanted, whatever desire he had, whatever whim took possession of him, he used his wealth freely for his own pleasure. But never for the happiness of any one else. He lived for self and only self.

It came to pass, as a matter of course, that as he grew to middle age he was a man without friends. In the village and thereabouts he was regarded very much as a stranger. The minister had long ago left him out of his books, for he had long ago withdrawn himself severely from all local associations, whether of church, or charity, or social life. In the city he was well known as a man of wealth, and had many acquaintances in the street and the clubs, but no friends. His intercourse with mankind, though outwardly cordial, with all the apparent friendliness which characterizes the surface of social and business life, was nevertheless purely formal, without heart or heartiness, and furnished no happiness for those solitary times when most men need something warm and cheery to think about. This man was no rare and peculiar specimen of humanity.

He was just what thousands of men are, of whom others say "he cares for nothing but business."

There had been a good deal of autumn work on the home farm, and he had superintended it, not going to town for several days. He had not been quite well. He had queer sounds in his ears and queer whirlings in his head. The week had been a succession of golden days, growing colder from day to day. It was nearly sunset, and he stood at the front window looking out over the landscape. The elm-trees which stood in front of the house were leafless. The road beyond them was dusty, and when a wagon went by clouds rose, reddened in the sunlight, and drifted out over the meadow on the other side of the road, where stood a group of his cattle waiting to be brought in to their night shelter. Beyond the meadow was the river, a noble stream, in which when he was a boy he had found trout plentiful, and, finding them, had found happiness.

He did not know why it was this evening that looking over there he remembered his boyhood, and it was strange to him to recall that kind of happiness which he then enjoyed. He had never been unhappy; he thought he had been on the whole a happy man; but just now there was a queer thrill of delight, for one little instant, in his mind, as if he were no longer a strong man of fifty, but that boy, with other boys, down yonder on the bank of the river. When that thrill passed away he somehow recognized that he was now quite far from being as happy as he was once.

The thought disturbed him, and he dismissed it impatiently, and turned to the side window, whence he looked down the road. There he saw the church and the church-yard behind it. There were no leaves on the intervening brush, and he could see, prominent among the stones, the monument which was over the graves of his father and his mother. He did not think of the words of just praise which were on the stone, and which all who knew them and all who did not know them could read. He thought of them as he knew them, and he couldn't help thinking of himself as they knew him. Thought is very swift. It takes but the time of a lightning-flash for one to review a long, a very long history. He saw them—his father, an honorable, God-fearing, neighbor-loving man, respected, loved, honored by all the people; his mother, a calm-eyed lovely lady, to whom the rich and the poor alike looked with assurance of sympathy in sorrow and help in distress. But chiefly he saw her as his mother, her look into his eyes, her exceeding beauty to him. How he loved, how he worshipped her! And how she loved him, him her boy! It was but a flash of memory, and again he was himself, the man grown, and moulded by a life unknown to his father and mother. When he was thus again himself he could not help thinking how great was the contrast between that old life and this in one respect, that now no one loved him. And that thought lingered.

He tried to laugh it away as sentimental. But it would not be laughed away. For it is a serious, solemn thought, involving all that concerns one's character and life. Not to have the love of any one, man or woman, boy or girl, is a terrible affliction, and most terrible to him who says he does not want it! For such saying argues that the man isn't worth loving, and therefore that the sooner he is under the sod and out of the way the sooner his place may be filled for the good of society.

He had never loved or been loved by any woman but his mother. So he now said to himself. And yet as he said it he turned from the window and, crossing the room, stood before a picture which hung on the wall. He possessed many superb pictures by renowned artists. There was an Old Crome, the envy of connoisseurs, a Gainsborough whose genuineness was not to be impeached, a Cuyp of exquisite beauty. There were a dozen other paintings in his room, landscapes and figure pieces, each of which was a gem. He had good taste, and had gratified it always. But he walked directly over to the place where was hanging a painting by an unknown artist, which he had bought simply because he liked it. He stood before it and looked into the face of a young country girl holding her apron full of wild flowers and shading her eyes from the sun with her uplifted hand.

He looked at that face but an instant. Perhaps there is no reason for the conjecture that that fair countenance resembled a face he had seen in the life. Perhaps it was a foolish fancy of his that if he ever met that girl in flesh and blood he could ask her to love him. Perhaps—but imagination here is vain.

He had stood there but a moment when the butler opened the folding-doors and announced that dinner was served. He dined alone as usual. His table shone with bright light on silver and old porcelain and glass. He sat facing the fireplace. Above it was the old wooden mantel-piece, its white front ornamented with charming reliefs, vases, and wreaths. The chairs were the ancient family chairs— heavy mahogany. The very fire-irons, with their brass mountings, the andirons, tongs, shovel, poker, all were the old irons handled by the old folks, and by himself when he was a boy in this room.

It was a struggle now to keep down memories, and he gave up the struggle and let them have their way, for they were rather cold memories and did not disturb him at the first. But they grew warmer as the solitary dinner progressed, and he began to ask himself why, on this particular evening, such a crowd of them pressed in on him. It was not till a little later that he knew. He was somewhat of an epicure. His servants knew his ways and what he liked, and he gave no orders for his meals. That was their business. Now as the butler lifted the cover from the silver soup-tureen he recalled the old time when the tureen was a mighty old Staffordshire vessel, cream white with bright green ruffled edge, and his mother filled the soup-plates for six children around the table, five daughters all dead long ago, and one son now dining here alone.

He remembered the face and form of Tacitus, the old colored butler of those days. He saw for a moment across the room the white-aproned Delia, wife of Tacitus, waiting to wait on Tacitus should need be. He saw all that was there forty years ago, and a very unpleasant dinner he had of it. For all this remembering of old times and early life was not to his liking. He had long ago moved out of that life and its relationships. It was his custom to drink at dinner only a sparkling table water, until he arrived at the fruit, when he always took his bottle of wine and finished it with his cigar. He drank usually a plain, sound Burgundy of medium grade, Macon or Pommard; but once in a while, say on New Year's Day or Fourth of July, he would take a higher grade of wine of the vineyards of gold, perhaps Romanée or Richebourg or Vougeot. For in his cellar he had ample stock of fine wines, which he used temperately.

It was a surprise to him when taking up his glass

of wine, which his servant had filled, and lifting it towards his lips he recognized the aroma of Vougeot.

"Why is this, Paolo?" he asked.

"I thought, sir, you would wish some good wine to-day."

"Why to-day?"

"Surely, sir, to-day is what you call Thanksgiving."

Thanksgiving Day! Hopeless now to struggle with those crowding memories. What man who was a Connecticut boy forty years ago can expel from his mind the memories of home on that day? He was not an emotional man. He gave no external sign of the internal tumult. He smoked his cigar and drank a single glass of wine, and thought, and thought, and thought. He left the table and walked into the front room, and sat in the large chair by the window, and looked out at the light of the full moon and thought. He lay back in his chair and looked across at that girl's picture, lit by a strong bar of light from the dining-room—that bright and beautiful face which looked back at him; and the riot of his thinking became tumultuous.

"The past," he said to himself, "was full of people, and the future will be full of people, and I am alone among them all. Alone! What have I ever done for any man or woman or child, any being in the universe, that that person should thank God that he made me; that that person should come up to me and say, 'I thank you'? Alone! I am alone now; and when I go where there is no buying and selling, and no one to care for me as a buyer or seller, I shall be absolutely alone. What is the currency of that country where my father and mother now are? Not gold or silver! What was that old song the mother used to sing in this very room?

"'There nectar and ambrosie spring; there musk and civet sweet;
There many a fair and dainty drug is trod down under feet.'

If I go there without money in my purse, wherewith am I to buy those dainties? Wherewith am I to buy the bread of life? What shall I live on? Why, the currency of that country is love. The bread of that life is love. So my mother told me. Have I any to carry with me when I go? Shall I find any one who has any to lend me, or pay me, or to give me there? Did I ever give a gift or do a good thing to any one, young or old, rich or poor—anything for which I did not expect, demand, and get full repayment? Does any one on earth, in heaven or hell, owe me one iota of kindness, gratitude, love? 'Lay up treasure; lay up treasure—' What was that advice I used to get from the old folks here?"

Vain were it to attempt an analysis of the crush and crash of thoughts which filled the brain and bewildered the intellect of the strong man, around whom were now gathering profound shadows. He sat there motionless. The servants cleared away the table in the other room, and wondered to see him sitting by the window in the dim light. They went away to their own part of the house, leaving him, as was their custom, to the solitary occupation of the great house. Towards midnight one of them came into the dining-room to put out the lights. He was still sitting there. When they came to lay the breakfast-table in the morning he was still there. Had his soul gone out beyond the November moonlight—out into the unknown light or unknown darkness, into the cold, shivering, alone?

No! Better, perhaps, if it had—or, at least, as well.

What visions, memories, imaginings, what penitences or what despairs, were in that imprisoned soul then and thereafter no one knows. The house is there, the pictures are there, the furniture, the fire-irons, the porcelains and glass and silver are there. But the sunshine never finds its way through the closed shutters. The wine is ripening in the cellar bins, but for whose lips no one can tell. The man himself is there, body and soul, in an upper room, in that mysterious condition, more mysterious than death, which forbids intelligent intercourse between an imprisoned mind and the world around it. But his great fortune, accumulating under the care of strangers, is just as useful to him and to his fellow-men—no less, no more—as it was when his fingers gathered the coins together, and grasped them and held them.

XII

HOW THE OLD LADY BEAT JOHN

We had been driving out some miles in the afternoon, and coming home in the twilight, passed a substantial-looking though very old farm-house, with comfortable barns and out-buildings, indicating a well-to-do householder. The rich bottom-lands, which stretched away a half-mile from the river to the hill-slopes, covered with abundant birch and maple, were luxuriant with grain and corn.

That evening, when we were sitting in the library, after dinner, smoking and chatting, I asked the Judge, "To whom does that farm we passed on the level belong?"

The Judge is not and never was on the bench. Yet long as I had known him, and that was a long time, he had been called "Judge" by all the country people, because it was an established fact of ancient date that he decided most of the disputes and differences, commercial and social, which arose in that part of the country. It is frequently the case, as here, that one man in a scattered community is the recognized adviser to whom people can go.

My old friend had inherited this position from his father, who had been to a former generation what the son now was to his neighbors. They came to him on all occasions when they needed counsel, and he did the work of a half-dozen lawyers. No one had died or could die comfortably and leave property unless his will had been drawn by "Judge ——." He had the perfect confidence of all. Living from youth up among them, known to be a man of extended education, whose life was passed in study, but who was also a practical farmer of great skill and success, having large property, and always giving his advice and services as a matter of friendship and neighborly kindness, and not for fee or reward, his position was one of commanding influence. His influence was commanding, too, for the reason that he almost never exerted it. He took no prominent part in politics; but in the old times there were very many voters in the town, and more in the county, who could give no other reason for their votes than this: that they voted as the Judge voted.

I have said that he drew the wills for people who had property. This was no small generosity, for it involved much time and often great inconvenience. But the Judge was an essential part of the social structure in that town, and quietly performed what he regarded as the duty and pleasure of his position.

When I asked him who was the owner of that

farm he laughed outright, and, after a moment's pause, said, "I will tell you a story.

"One stormy winter night, after midnight, I was sitting here reading, the rest of the family having gone to sleep long before, when old Dr. Strong thundered at the door-knocker, and made noise enough to wake the Seven Sleepers. It is a way he has, and neither my wife nor the girls, who were roused out of slumber, nor I myself, had any question who was at the door. I let him in myself, and a tempest of wind and snow with him. The blast that drove him into my arms also put out the hall lights, whirled into the library, and flared the reading-lamp so that it broke the chimney and blazed up to a colored tissue-paper affair which Susie had put over the shade, set it on fire, and for a moment threatened a general conflagration of papers and books on the table.

"'Shut the door yourself!' I shouted, and rushed in here to put out the fire. That done, I went back and found the old doctor out of breath, in the dark, trying to shut the door against the wind. It took the strength of both of us to do it. Then I told him to find his way to the library, for he knew it, and I went off in search of another lamp.

"When I came back he was just recovering his wind, and, after a gasp or two, told me his errand. 'Old Mrs. Norton is dying. She can't live till morning. She's alive now only on stimulants.

She wants to make a will, and I have come for you.'

"'A nice night,' I said, 'for a two-mile drive, to make a will for a woman who hasn't a cent in the world to leave. Why didn't you tell her so, and have done with it.'

"'Now look here,' said the doctor, 'this is a case of an old woman and old neighbor and friend, and she wants you to do something for her, and you'll do it, if it's only to comfort her last hours. Get your things and come with me. We shall not find her alive if you don't hurry, and you'll be sorry if that happens.'

"The upshot of it was that I went. We had a fearful drive out to the farm-house on the flat, which you are asking about. Mrs. Norton was the widow of John Norton, who had died forty odd years before this. John Norton when he married her was a widower with one son—John. He was a man of considerable property, and when he died left a widow, that son John by his first wife, and two sons by his second wife. The elder son, John, had never been on very warm terms with his step-mother, and for some years had had no intercourse with the family.

"I found the old lady lying in the big room, on a great bedstead on one side of the room, opposite to the broad chimney, in which was a roaring fire, the only light in the room. After the doctor had spoken to her and administered something—a stimulant, I suppose—he came over to me and said in a whisper: 'Hurry up; she's very weak.'

"I had brought paper and pen and ink with me. I found a stand and a candle, placed them at the head of the bed, and, after saying a few words to her, told her I was ready to prepare the will, if she would now go on and tell me what she wanted to do. I wrote the introductory phrase rapidly, and, leaning over towards her, said: 'Now go on, Mrs. Norton.' Her voice was quite faint, and she seemed to speak with an effort. She said: 'First of all I want to give the farm to my sons Harry and James; just put that down.' 'But,' said I, 'you can't do that, Mrs. Norton; the farm isn't yours to give away.'

"'The farm isn't mine?' she said, in a voice decidedly stronger than before.

"'No; the farm isn't yours. You have only a life interest in it.'

"'This farm, that I've run for goin' on forty-three year next spring, isn't mine to do what I please with it! Why not, Judge? I'd like to know what you mean!'

"'Why, Mr. Norton, your husband, gave you a life estate in all his property, and on your death the farm goes to his son John, and your children get the village houses. I have explained that to you very often before.'

"'And when I die John Norton is to have this house and farm, whether I will or no?'

"'Just so. It will be his.'

"'Then I ain't going to die!' said the old woman, in a clear and decidedly ringing and healthy voice. And, so saying, she threw her feet over the front of the bed, sat up, gathered a blanket and coverlet about her, straightened up her gaunt form, walked across the room, and sat down in a great chair before the fire.

"The doctor and I came home. That was fifteen years ago. The old lady's alive to-day. And she accomplished her intent. She beat John, after all. He died four years ago, in Boston, and I don't know what will he left. But whoever comes into the farmhouse when she goes out, it will not be John. And since John's death the farm has been better kept, and everything about it is in vastly better condition for strangers than it would have been for John."

XIII

PHILISTIS

We were sitting by the fire after breakfast. The dominie was thinking. I was turning over a pile of old newspapers and wondering why he had kept them.

"That paper," said he, "I kept because it had a letter from Sicily, speaking of a beautiful coin of Philistis. It is engraved in Visconti. Did you ever see it?"

"See it, man? Yes; did I never show it to you?"

"Show what?"

"That coin of Philistis. I first saw it thirty years ago, fell in love with it as the most beautiful head produced by Greek art in die-cutting that I ever saw, and I never have parted with it. I know a woman who looks like that face of the Sicilian queen."

So saying, I took the silver coin from its little envelope in my pocket-case, and handed it to him. Whoever has seen that silver tetradrachm knows the beauty of that head of Philistis.

My friend was more silent than before. He held

the coin in his hand, and buried his gaze into it for some space of time.

"Yes, I thought so; but the Greek engraver was far ahead of the modern who attempted a copy. He knew her, he loved her, if she was a queen. And this is she. I thought I knew her. Yes, it is she."

"You knew her too. Where did you know—"

"No, no, my friend. It has been said that God never makes persons of different generations exactly alike. That is not true. There was one Philistis in old times. You knew another. I knew a third, and she might have been a resurrection in the body of this Sicilian woman. Come with me."

The library opened out at its side to a little gate entering the church-yard, and he led me to a grave, by which he paused and said, "My Philistis is here."

Then, leaning on the head-stone while I leaned on another, the smoke of our cigars ascending in the still October air, the sunshine glittering on maple-leaves that fell through the brilliant light, one by one, on graves around us, he talked.

"She was born in that old house over yonder. When I met you in Jerusalem in 1856 she was a child of ten years old. When I came home and saw her again I thought she was the loveliest child for beauty of face and beauty of mind I had ever known. I have seen many since, and I think so still. She has lain here quietly enough for fifteen years. The first rest she ever had, after her girlhood was over, she found here.

"What a woman she was at nineteen! Till then her life was sunny; after that it was all cloud and storm. What she looked like, judge by your coin. She had not much companionship here of her own grade of mind, but there were three or four daughters of neighbors within the ten-mile stretch of my parish who went to school with her, and afterwards they begged me to give them lessons. And they grew up fond of reading and fond of art history, and their visits to New York and Albany were full of incident and opened their minds; and she went once to Europe for a year with her aunt, and once to Cuba and Mexico with her father. I don't exactly like that word 'cultivated,' for she was far ahead of what you ordinarily mean by a cultivated woman. I can't tell you what a light she was to us in the old parsonage. My daughter was younger than she, and owes all she is to the rare example of perfect womanhood, self-trust, and self-respect which that dear girl showed her.

"She had troubles beginning to surround her life when she was nineteen. You can judge of the courage with which she was likely to meet all the troubles of this world by what once happened under my own eyes.

"You see over there across the valley, where the

river comes out of the glen? It runs deep and strong through the ravine, and rushes out to the level land through a narrow gorge. We had gone out there to look for a rare fern. Botanizing was a favorite play for us. We were five or six. I with my horse and buckboard took one of the girls. She and the others were on horseback. It was in August. We had left the horses, and were searching up the banks of the river. I was standing on the ridge of rock, fifty feet above the river. She had gone below me up a narrow ledge along the stream, three or four feet above and close over the edge of the swift water. A few bushes clung there and lay out over the stream. Suddenly I heard a cry of horrible distress. I looked down to her instinctively. She was all right, but she too had heard it, and was looking up-stream. Then my eyes followed hers, and twenty rods above I saw a twelve-year-old boy on a rock gesticulating and yelling. In the river, rolling and plunging down the rapid, was a bundle of something. It turned out afterwards to be his little brother, who had rolled off the rock into the river. She told me afterwards she had seen them a moment before, and knew it was the child.

"It took just about thirty seconds for that bundle of clothes to come swift as an arrow down to us. Knowing the girl as well as I did, my only thought was that she would do something rash, and I looked at her steadily and wished for wings to drop myself down to her side.

"Now I will tell you what I saw her do. I saw her measure with her eye the course of the current and the direction of the child's sweep. Then she measured the depth of the water at the foot of the ledge she was standing on, and, seeing bottom, not very deep, she sat down on the ledge and deliberately slid down, feet first, into the water, and stood up straight and firm, and seized the trunk-stem of a bush that lay out over the water. Then, without looking away from the child, she sent out a clear ringing call for help, that went over the rocks in spite of the river's noise. By this time I was halfway down the steep, and I answered her. The child was coming towards the upper side of the bush. I thought it was safe to strike there. So did she. But at the last moment a swirl sent the little one off shore, just into the end of the bush, and as it caught and swung once around there and was going away to death, she threw herself quietly—I say quietly, for it was a graceful motion — forward on her face, plunged her right hand into the mass of branches and grasped them, while with her left she seized the clothes of the child. Her feet swung out down-stream, the water boiled over her shoulders and face, but she held on with both grasps, and the bush swayed down and in shore just in time for me to seize her and draw them both ashore. No, I didn't draw them ashore. She touched bottom with her feet, and when she felt my grasp on her clothes let go the bush, took my hand, and stood up in the water, and I got them both ashore somehow.

"That's the stuff some of our Northern women are made of. Gentle, lovable, full of all purity; taught all graces by the beauty which surrounded her life; unspotted of the world; ah, my animadulcis, no love of man ever stained thy sweet soul!

"I could have placed here the sad epitaph of Julia Alpinella:

"'*Hic jaceo, infelicis patris infelix proles; exorare patris necem non potui; male mori in fatis ille erat; vixi annos* XXIII.'"

I did not ask nor did my friend relate to me any of the story which is summed up in that (perhaps fabulous) old epitaph of a servant of Diana, and of a modern New England girl. Was it not Byron, or who was it, that said it was the saddest story ever told on a memorial tablet?

When I went to my room that night I missed the coin. Next morning he said he had looked at it three times in the night, when he woke, restless from dreams, and—and—did I value it very much? Would I let him show it to just two ladies, who knew and loved his Philistis? Yes, I would, and therefore he might keep it, but only till we meet again, for did not I too know a fair woman whose face was that of the queen of Hiero? But his Philistis was dead, and mine lives yet; he loved his Philistis as his own child, and I but admired the one I knew as a beautiful woman. But then the more reason I should have it. For the living change, and as they change they imperceptibly efface our memories of what they were; and so a thing of beauty is not a joy forever, unless it be like the silver stamp of the Greek gem-engraver's die.

"But you, my friend, you remember that face; you haven't forgotten it?"

"Never, never, but I want this. Get another for yourself. Leave this one here. Have a portrait painted of your Philistis. Get a sculptor to do her in marble. She is no such woman as was our little one, the light of our eyes."

Could I resist him? Don't we all of us have that same feeling that those we have loved and lost were far more lovely than those any one else has loved and lost?

XIV

A NORTHERN SLEIGH-RIDE

WHEN Christmas-time approaches, young people grow merry, and old people, if they are right-minded, should grow calmly happy. We who have kept Christmas festivals for many years, so that we can count back one after another of them for a half-hundred and more, ought to have laid up a store of pleasant things to think about. If we have not done so it is time to begin.

On Monday the snow fell nineteen inches deep, and all the country is white for the joyous festival. Christmas without snow is unknown to our memories, who were brought up in the north country. Sitting before the fire a little while ago, there came into my thoughts a group of faces which were so full of bright, overflowing joy, and the beauty of youth and hope, that I am half convinced every one of them, wherever they are, in this or another world, has lighted up with memory of the same scene.

It was in the Christmas holiday vacation. I was at home from college. I am not sure now whether in those days they gave us a Christmas vacation in Princeton, but I know that I went home. I remember getting up early in the cold winter morning, taking the stage, and dragging through deep mud to New Brunswick, where we, a lot of New York boys, took steamboat down the Raritan and up the bay to New York. The Philadelphia Railroad was then running, with small, old-fashioned coaches for cars. But the railroad fares were high, and the students from New York knew how to save a dollar or two out of their allowances by taking stage and steamboat. I went up the Hudson, to my home above the Highlands, in an evening boat. The river had remained open that year much later than usual. Next day began the Christmas jollities; but it is one evening's adventures which arrest my memories to-night.

It was a brilliant, cold afternoon when Joe S—— came to hunt me up and propose a sleigh-ride. There was to be a grand convention of some society that evening at a town fifteen miles up the river. It was always easier in those days for daughters to persuade their mothers to let them go on a sleigh-ride to a certain place and meeting than to go on a sleigh-ride pure and simple. And then, any great meeting—religious, moral, or sensational—was a far greater event than now in the rural districts.

"But where can we get a team, Joe?" I said. "Our horses are gone off."

"Your father's big sleigh hasn't gone?"

"No."

"Then I'll tell you what I propose. Mr. Staunton is in New York. His sorrels haven't been out for a week. He lets you drive them. You get them. I'll bring around my father's bays and our farm harness. We'll hitch them to your big sleigh. It'll make a glorious team."

"But who will drive them? None of them were ever harnessed four-in-hand. If I'm going for a sleigh-ride with the girls, I'm not going to give all my time to tooling a new team like that, I can tell you."

"That's all fixed. Steve will be here in fifteen minutes with old Cæsar, and Cæsar can drive anything that ever went in harness."

Boys were boys then, and will be boys forever. I thank God devoutly that there are yet hours in which I know that I am a boy; and always about Christmas-time the boy-spirit comes back and asserts its omnipotence over care and responsibility and sorrow and years.

There was no thought in any of our young heads of the risk, the danger to the precious load we intended to take. The prospect of a glorious moonlight sleigh-ride, four boys, four girls, and any married couple we could get to go along (to do propriety), this shut out all thought except of how to get off. But there was a very doubtful point, in which, as I grew older—in fact, before I was four hours older—I became convinced my boy enthusiasm had led me to do wrong. I do not tell the story for boys' imitation. I cannot make a moral to the story by relating a catastrophe as the fitting punishment for our wrong-doing. All went off with superb success. But, my boys, if one of you read this, don't go and do so. It was only next door to horse-stealing. That is fact. For I knew that Joe's father would never trust that pair of bays in any hands but his own. They were splendid animals, and he and Mr. Staunton were forever matching one another with their favorite teams. I knew also that although Mr. Staunton had often trusted me with those powerful sorrels, he would not be very likely to let me or any one put them in a four-horse team, especially with those bays. However, I left Joe to settle his own conscience and bring the horses, while I went over to Mr. Staunton's stable, took the sorrels from his coachman, who thought it must be all right, and asked no questions.

We had a time of it getting them into harness. Cæsar was full of ecstasy over the prospect. The old colored man knew horses all by heart, and knew boys too. He understood the entire performance, and he wanted the fun as much as we, and suggested no difficulties; but he looked to the harness with all his old eyes. Cæsar had some confidence in me, boy though I was, and he whispered to me:

"You're going to sit by me on the box-seat, Mr. W——, ain't you?"

While the harnessing was going on I had gone into the house and asked my elder brother and his wife to go with us, and obtained their assent. Better company for such a ride no boys and girls on earth could have had.

When all was ready, my brother came out and joined us. Joseph and Stephen and my brother piled into the sleigh. Cæsar took the reins on the high front seat. I sat by him. The sun was just on the horizon. The flush of sunset was over the whole country, covered deep with two feet of snow on a level, and drifts six and ten feet high wherever the wind had eddied or dropped a light fleece. It was forty rods from our carriage-house to the street gate and the turn into the road. It was three-quarters of a mile up the road to the fork, then half a mile down the other road to the two houses, where we had sent Philip P—— to ask our four young friends to be ready.

Two men who stood at the leaders' heads (the bays were on the lead) let go, and the team sprang forward. Then, for just a moment, the sorrels threatened to balk, and the off horse stood up and struck out his fore-feet at the bay leader. The nigh sorrel had intended to go all right, but at that he struck the dash-board with his iron heels, and stretched his head down and out as if he wanted to fight. The whole team was almost in a tangle for the instant, but the next they were straining steadily on the tugs, and we were going for the gate.

"Sit down!" I shouted to my companions, who were all standing up and holding by the back of the box-seat and one another, watching the horses. They paid no heed. We went through the gate, and as we went through it I saw that Cæsar hadn't force enough in his old left arm to swing that mighty team up the road. I seized the reins above his hands, and with all my strength, added to his, the horses yielded, the leaders plunging through the snow on the opposite side of the beaten track in the main road, the wheelers swinging in the track, the sleigh, like a stone in a sling, hurled around and rising on one runner, with the other high in the air. Do you know what a catapult is? A sleigh swinging as that sleigh swung, and fetching up with a sudden shock in the track, is a catapult. I did not know that Stephen had been shot into a snowdrift, for Cæsar went away from my side like a dark shell from a mortar. Wide-awake Cæsar! He didn't hold on to the reins. I was alone on the box, the broad straight road before me, and the horses going not quite so swift as the rays of the red sunset which shot right up the road.

The beaten track was narrow, but the road was broad and level. It is generally an easy matter to stop a runaway team under such circumstances, and I followed the rule. The leaders yielded to a steady strain, and the wheelers followed them into the deep snow. A few rods of that was enough for them. They brought up, trembling and frightened at their own doings. A few kind words and touches did them good, while Stephen and Cæsar overtook us, with sundry sleigh-robes that had gone out with them. When we reached the fork of the roads we had gotten up too much steam for a turn down the sharp angle, and went a mile farther, around a square, and back. By the time we came in front of the house of that dear old lady whose daughters we proposed first to pick up, the team was calm enough to stand without any of us at their heads. Fortunate that, for she never would have let the girls go if she had seen any of the events of the previous fifteen minutes. I see I have called her an old lady. That is another illustration of the ever-persistent boyhood in us. I should call one of her age a young lady now. She was the beautiful mother of two beautiful daughters, and the three were like three sisters in appearance.

If one were to write out the memories of one such day and evening, as they crowd in on him when he deliberately invites them in, he could fill a volume.

Our company was made up, and the short twilight had changed into the white light of a winter moon, nearly full, when we were off for a fifteen-mile stretch, up hill and down, over a glassy road.

Sleigh-riding by moonlight was, in our younger days, the most exhilarating of all pleasures. It is difficult to explain why it was so. The social enjoyments of the young in winter—evening gatherings, receptions, dancing-parties, balls—are more or less attractive to different dispositions. But I never knew one young person yet, in good health, who would not give up any ball or any conceivable social enjoyment for a sleigh-riding party by moonlight. And I think it fair to say that the underlying reason for this is in the innate love of the beautiful, the pure, the holy, which most, if not all, young people possess. No wealth of flowers, no lavish expenditure of art on the adornment of a ball-room, surrounds the young heart with such beauty and glory as the winter snow light, and in no life that art and wealth can create do pure young souls find their native atmosphere of purity, to which they were born, and in which alone they breathe freely. A moonlight night in a snow-covered country, if it be not nearer the light of heaven than any other earthly light, is at least more unearthly than any other, for in such illuminated nights we see only the glory and nothing of the vileness of this life.

I cannot linger on that ride in these pages. You who never took a sleigh-ride would like to know how the time was passed as we flew like the wind along the road. Well, we were all a fairly educated lot of young people. There was a pretty steady rattle of talk and story and joke and riddles, and now and then a song. Was there any chance for a quiet talk— just one with one? Obviously there was, for sleigh-bells on four swift horses fill the air with noise, and that makes confidential talk as easy as a balcony, or a conservatory, or any such place of escape from a ball-room. Did I enjoy it, up there on the box-seat with old Cæsar? Bless your soul, my dear young lady, I didn't sit next to Cæsar after we started. There was some one between us with a lovely face! such eyes! such hair! such a little pair of hands! little even in their fur gloves. And those little hands were constantly aching to get hold of those reins; and once, when the team came down to a walk half-way up a hill, Cæsar let them hold the hurricane till we reached the top. All that winter I wrote poetry about those same eyes and that face and those hands, and I could have referred you to the poetry in print, if the editors of the *Nassau Monthly* had not refused to recognize its value.

I must hurry on. We drove to the hotel in the large village, ordered supper, and, to make a proper report to the mothers at home, went for ten minutes to the meeting. I wish I could remember what it was about. I don't; and I don't think I knew then, though it was in a large church, and we found a large audience.

But I do know and have never forgotten that when we had been standing five minutes behind the back pews near the doors, where many were standing, and we were looking over the heads of the people at some one who was firing away on a platform in front of the pulpit, I felt a hand on my shoulder, and, looking around, met the eyes of my father's friend, Mr. Staunton, owner of the sorrel horses.

For an instant I was—well, there is no word to explain the exact sensation. If one were writing a French novel he would say he nearly fainted, he was "bouleversed," he was—any exaggeration you please. But this is plain fact, and the fact is that American boys in those days were never much taken aback by the unexpected, which was then, as now, always happening. What came nearer to causing a violation of the proprieties of a meeting in a church by a shout of laughter was the pressure on my wrist of one of those little hands, now ungloved, and the despairing countenances of the whole party. It was lucky that they were all near enough together to see and hear what passed. In a low voice Mr. Staunton said:

"I'm glad to see you. I came up in the boat from New York, and instead of stopping at home I thought I would come on up to the meeting, on the chance of finding some one here and getting a ride home. How did you come here? Can you take me down?"

"Oh yes, certainly; just as well as not; we've got a big sleigh and four horses; come to the hotel after the meeting. We're going there now for supper."

He went up the aisle. He was a delegate, or a director, or something or other. He was a grand good man, and we young people all were very fond of him. We went out. What fun we had at supper, and what a burst of merriment would come once in a while as we arranged for taking our good friend Mr. Staunton home behind his own horses "unbeknownst" to him! But we solemnly pledged ourselves to each other that if we succeeded, we would never whisper the story to any human being so long as he lived. And we did it, and we kept the pledge. He lived to a good old age and died only three years ago, and last summer at Lonesome Lake I told the story for the first time to his nephew.

The horses came to the hotel door. The girls surrounded him, and talked and hustled him into the sleigh first of all, because he was our invited guest and must be best cared for. That was the moment of chief danger, for he was a lover of horses, and had a way of walking around and looking at a team. That team was worth looking at! I changed seats with Cæsar. There was no telling what might happen, and the way to be ready for the unexpected is to expect everything.

The team was fresh now, and the moon was as

bright as ever. I had almost forgotten the overhanging trouble as the sleigh swept along the white track behind those magnificent animals. Suddenly there was silence behind me where had been a babel of voices. They were appalled, and saw no way to avoid what seemed to be an inevitable revelation. "Why didn't you pull his feet out from under him and tumble over him, and get up a general scrimmage," I afterwards asked Joe. "I was too scared to think of anything when I saw him stand up and take hold of the box-seat and look at those horses," frankly confessed my poor Joe. The next moment I heard a voice close to my ear.

"I didn't think there was a pair of horses in the country that could step so like my sorrels. Whose are they, W——?"

Before the words were out the loose white snow at the road-side was flying from the heels of the leaders, over the sorrels, into his face, over the sleigh; the trot was broken into a short, plunging gallop, the right runner, off the track, was ploughing deep in the unbeaten white, and most of the people in that sleigh were expecting an upset. Two of them, on the front seat, expected no such thing, for out of a sable fur hood at my left came a quick cry, and, "Oh, Mr. Staunton, do sit down, you nearly threw me out; make him sit down."

And down he went, into all their arms, for Joe had come to his senses by this time. Then they all made much of him for an hour, and got him to telling stories, and all went bravely on till we approached home.

"We'll drop you at the corner, Mr. Staunton; stand ready to jump." And out he went; the horses came down to a slow gait without stopping; and among those trees in that light he couldn't tell a sorrel from an iron-gray, as we rushed away to the village.

There were no bells about those horses when about three o'clock in the morning I led them myself into their stable. I woke the coachman, who slept in the carriage-house, and enjoined on him perpetual silence, sealed with silver, more—much more—than I had saved by coming from Princeton to New York in the stage and steamboat.

Yes, boys; that's the only thing in this story worth your remembering. Doing wrong mostly must be paid for; and a dime in those days, to a country boy, was bigger than a dollar is now. But what a night that was! The moon has grown much paler since those times. This is a true story. Witness my hand.

XV

LIFE SEEN THROUGH A WINDOW

THERE was nothing remarkable about the appearance of the house. It was old and weather-colored; that is, having been built of wood and never painted, a gray-brown tint had come over all the wood, perhaps fifty years ago, and remained unchanged. For if any boards had at any time been removed, those replacing them had soon taken the same tint. It was but one story high, and there were four rooms on the floor. A very ancient block-house, the original home of the family, adjoined it, and was still useful, part of it as the dairy and part as the woodshed.

There were old trees a little way from the house, but none shaded it. On each side of the door, which was in the middle of the long side, and fronted the road, was a group of bushes, I am not sure what. They partly shaded the broad stone door-step, and also shaded the windows nearest the door on each side. It was through one of these that I caught sight of her face. The glass was that queer old twisted, uneven, shining, and iridescent glass that one never sees nowadays, but which was the only kind used in country-houses in old times. It had its smooth, transparent spots, and the occupants of houses, especially the young people, always learned the exact location of those available spots, and went straight to them to look out, unless they were content with distorted views of nature.

Many times, driving by, I had seen that face through that same window, and at length it happened that I had occasion to see the man of the house on some business about a horse, and so it came that one day when I asked him a question about the neighborhood, he said, " My mother could tell that; you never saw her; come in and see her." And so I went into the room on the south side, and saw the face without the intervening glass. It was a face of wonderful beauty. She was a very old lady, and for almost or quite fifty years had been an invalid, unable to walk, moved daily from her bed in the adjoining room to her chair by that window, and removed at night to her bed again. Her mind was clear and active, her body sadly ill and suffering. She had never been out of those rooms for half a century. The world seen through one window for fifty years might well have a peculiar aspect. And as I often afterwards stopped to see and talk with her, I had some curiosity to know what this aspect was to her vision.

If you imagine that she had seen but little of it

you are mistaken. The experiences of life which make up what we call "the world" are more varied perhaps in great cities, but the impressions they' make are deeper in the country. And through that window she had seen very much, and what she had seen had entered into her soul. I cannot enumerate them—not a tenth or a hundredth part of the things she saw. I need not speak of the recurrence of the seasons, the coming of springs on meadows and hills, and the white coverings of winters, the growth of great trees from young saplings, the coming into the fields and along the fences and walls of new foliage and new flowers, the successive crops on the lowlands across the road, and the generations of cattle and sheep that grazed in the pastures. All these she knew, and as her children were living and dutiful they had always taken care that she saw all that it was possible she could see. Though her eyes had never seen the new barns and stocksheds to the north of the house, every horse and ox and cow and calf, I think every lamb on the farm, had been shown to her through that window-pane. One day while I sat with her I saw the collie dog look up and smile at her through the glass, and she nodded to him, and he went on satisfied.

She was a widow when sickness first seized on her, and was ill very long before she could be brought out to the window. The first sight she saw there was the funeral of her father, and that scene she remembered vividly as the beginning of her views of life through the window. His neighbors carried him out of the door and down the walk to the gate, and laid him in the old box-wagon, and took him away. After that many of the beloved things of the world passed out of her view just there. She had four sons, and one of them she saw carried away just so. Her daughter's wedding made gay the green in front of the house. One by one, in after-years, she saw grandchildren come in at the gate, first babies brought in arms, then toddling children, glad to come to see her, then romping boys, never rough or rude in her presence, then stout young men, vigorous and full of life, and graceful girls, and every one of them most loving and tender to her. There was never one of them who did not enjoy sitting on the footstool by her side and talking to her, and telling her all their hearts' delights and anxieties. Somehow that room was a safe treasury for the deposit of young folks' secrets, and what was placed there was safe and never stolen or betrayed. Her youngest son, years ago, she saw turn back at the gate and wave his hand to her as he went away, and again and again at intervals of years she saw him coming in, each time bringing new honors that he had won, and him too she saw at last brought in by other hands to rest a little in the old home, and taken out again through the gate whither she had seen many that she loved go and many carried.

If the effect of such views of life be always the same it would be well for all of us to spend our lives behind the old-fashioned panes of window-glass. There was no distortion in the vision of my good old friend. Cheery and always bright, she had a clear judgment of persons, sound appreciation of character, abundant content, and her life had been, she said, and she proved it by her visible life, full of enjoyment. She always saw the bright side. Even the deepest afflictions, added to her one constant affliction, failed to destroy that ineffable calm and peace of mind in which she lived. Books she had read in great number, but mostly she read her Bible, and the visions she had through her window, whether of joy or grief, were alike interpreted to her and commented on by the philosophy which is above all human reason.

Hers had been a life worth living. We who think we see things through no clouds or mist or refracting medium, are far from seeing as clearly as did she. In all the country around she was a centre of good and benevolent influences. She knew all the people, young and old. So that when she at last went away the whole country mourned. She died in the late summer.

The ending was very pleasant. For a little she became a child again—not childish, but just a little child; so, at least, it seemed to those who cared for her.

She was sitting just there in the morning of a warm day. She had been very silent that morning; at least, so her grandson told me afterwards, but it may have been only an imagination. She was never talkative, and, unlike some old persons, she was wont to listen and smile her reply instead of speaking. So when a child of three years old, playing on the grass before the house, looked up into her face, and, holding up a bunch of flowers, shouted something to her, she only smiled and said nothing. Then the child repeated her question in a child's dictatorial way, and now the smile was very sweet that stole over the thin white features, and at the same time a far-away gaze was seen in her eyes. I say "was seen," for her grandson, a man of forty, coming in at the gate just then, was so struck by that gaze that he turned around and looked up the bend of the valley road, thinking she saw persons coming, and was trying to recognize them at a distance.

"There is no one on the road that I can see, grandmother," he said as he entered the door and turned into her room.

But there was some one on the road up which she was looking, with her face close to the pane of glass.

Not to eyes purely human is it given to see those who travel that road; but many times the aged, sometimes the young, are permitted for a while, before the silver cord is quite loosened, to look with superhuman vision along the road which the angels and spirits of the just use in going to and fro between this and their country. How many of them she saw no one knows, but that she saw two at least cannot be doubtful. For just now her grandson approached her chair and heard her voice. She was murmuring to herself, and over and over again, smiling all the time, she was saying, "Joshua, Joshua, Susy, Susy."

Not far away from the farm there is an old graveyard, in which is a brown stone with two half-circle elevations on the top, and that one stone tells of the death of Joshua and Susan, twin children, in the year 1787. They were her brother and sister, a little older than she. When she was three years old they died at six. It is not likely that on this earth there was any other human being remaining whom those children had known and loved, or who had known and loved them. Had they waited all these long years for the coming of their baby sister? As they waited and watched, did she seem to them, from year to year, to grow older and less fair and beautiful than they had left her in the freshness of infancy? Were they ever weary of waiting? Do they keep count of days and years in the country whose light is perpetual and unchanging? Was she always a child to them grown strong in the atmosphere of Paradise?

Doubtless she, who alone of all the living could

have memory of those names thus coupled together in tones of affection, saw them on the road along which her mysterious vision was directed. After that she seemed to see no earthly scenes; and when they carried her out of the sunshine the smile did not leave her face, or if for a brief time it was not there, it came again with great beauty. She did not speak again. All that day she lay calm and quiet, and her company was evidently of the other sort of people, of whom we, so long as we are wholly human, know little and can imagine little. The evening drew on. The birds sang in the maples until the cry of the nighthawk alone was heard in the twilight. Then over on the hill-side whippoor-wills called mournfully to one another as the night went along. At midnight her grandson, the clergyman, arrived from his distant home. He looked for a little while at her beautiful face, spoke but received no reply, then knelt by the bed and repeated the words of the Lord's Prayer. He did not use the blundering form of the new revision, but the old phrases with which for so long time she had been familiar. As the sound reached her ears —that sound which seemed to be in the language of the other country, which Joshua and Susy understood, and in which they joined—her lips moved as if syllabling the words, but no sound came from them : nor after that.

XVI

COLORED PEOPLE

INTELLIGENT minds are seeking with great sincerity the solution of the problem : What is to be the future of the colored race in our country? And many are seeking it in great blindness. The governing white race in the Northern States are in general as ignorant of the character, the qualities, the abilities and disabilities of the colored race as they are of the character of the Afghans.

I am not speaking now of how little Northern men know about the colored race in the Southern States. I refer to the knowledge which whites in New England, New York, and elsewhere have of the colored people in their own states and towns and villages.

Political excitement and the wiles of politicians for the past forty years have kept the Southern colored man in sight so constantly that the Northern colored man has sunk out of sight. That kind of philanthropy which many delight in, forming societies, making speeches, collecting other people's money to spend, has found ample field in distant parts of the country, and the charity which ought to begin at home has not had its beginning.

There is more need to-day of Northern people recognizing the condition of the Northern colored man than of bothering about the Southern colored man. The colored race in the North is more neglected by Northerners, more isolated, set apart by the dominant sentiment of the whites than the colored race at the South by white Southerners.

The relations between the two races at the South are more Christian, more favorable to the elevation of the colored man, than at the North.

These are strong statements, but I write them deliberately and with knowledge. I could fill volumes with what I am confident would interest some readers, records of my personal acquaintance with Northern colored people, their homes, their employments and enjoyments, their social gatherings, their mutual benefit efforts, literary and other clubs and societies, their marriages, their funerals, and especially their religious associations in churches. It is pitiable beyond expression to see how utterly alone and unaided they are.

The colored people of the Northern States are, in fact, more "looked down on" by Northern whites than are the Southern freemen by Southern whites. This is no sweeping statement that I make without observation. Look around you, my friend, wherever you live, and consider the subject. What do you do for colored people? What is your mental method of regarding them? What do you know about the race in your city? Did you ever try to help them in any of their efforts to help themselves?

There are good people at the North who are living in complete self-satisfaction that with the abolition of slavery in the South they have done a glorious work, and all that they need do for the colored race in all the states, North and South. And all the time, at their doors, close around them, the race is living, a dependent people, unaided, uncared for, disregarded. There is plenty of work for the philanthropy of the North among Northern colored people.

The struggle of the colored people of the North for their own improvement and general advance is one of the deepest interest, full of pathos, because so patient and so unaided. Brought up in my babyhood and childhood by the hands of colored people, watched in my boyhood and youth by dark faces that I loved as well as any white faces, I have all my life been closely attached to many colored folk. How many Northerners who read this were ever at the wedding of a colored young man and woman, the baptism of a colored child, a social gathering of colored people, a meeting of a literary society of colored young men? How many of you ever cheered a respectable colored family by a friendly call—not a visit of patronage, but one of good-will and neighborliness? How many of you ever went, where all are free to go, to the funeral of a colored person? Do you say you were never invited on any such occasions? Why not? Did you ever give indication that you would accept an invitation? Would you go, if invited, except as a matter of curiosity? Those people, as a class throughout the North, live always conscious that you don't want their invitations, that you don't purpose to associate with them on any terms of any kind which may imply equality. Equality! The word is one of the humbugs of our age. It is the name of an imagination, a condition that has no existence in social and community life. In many a group of white men and women in society there are some (and you know them when you meet them) who are fitter for the State Prison than for your companionship; some who are immeasurably below others in moral, intellectual, physical, and other considerations. You are not going to make people your equals, black or white, by treating them as your "neighbors" in the highest authoritative sense of that word.

Legislation about hotels and railways will never produce equality. That will always be an individual question, dependent on influences far above the reach of law. You can no more legislate a man into society which rejects him than you can legislate railway and stock swindlers out of society which accepts them.

Don't imagine me seeking to abolish distinctions of the races, and bring about even apparent equality. I don't believe in it, don't want it, don't believe all the philanthropy on earth will or ought to accomplish it. Educated in the Westminster Catechism, I would have all men taught their duties in their several places and relations as "superiors, inferiors, and equals"—places and relations which will exist for all eternity, here and hereafter; without which the world would stagnate on a dead level of imbecility. But the superior owes duties of kindness, assistance, protection, education, sympathy, love to the inferior.

Yes, that is the word, love. I know—or I should say I have known, for all of them have gone to God and rank now as he ranks his chosen, in various lustre—I have known black men whom I loved, to whose lives of faithfulness, in their humble stations, I look back with affection, to whose graves my thoughts go, in wakeful night-times, as they often go to the graves of the beloved dead.

It was but a short time ago that one of them died. He was a servant, but more than a servant, steward of the entire household, of family interests, and a large part of the financial affairs, trusted and faithful, respected, honored—I use the word again—loved, by the old, by the children, by every one. The house was in one of our most wealthy cities. Few men in the city were more widely known or respected by the community, rich and poor. His fine form, his speaking countenance, his intelligent eye, all made him a man of mark. He was a gentleman in every sense of the word—in manner, habit, kindliness to those whom he could help, and he helped many in higher stations than his own. His intellectual ability and his intelligence were above those of the average of the people of the city. He was honored and trusted by the colored population. He was a free giver according to his small ability in charities and in his church, in which he held the most responsible position as a layman.

I have no space to dwell on the beauty of his character, which made us all love him. He was a child in his simplicity of faith, while he was a man in his unbending integrity. We never thought of the household as existing without him. When he was struck down by sudden illness, we had a revelation of the social conditions of the colored people in the city which astonished us. He was a member of a society. From the moment of his attack his associates devoted themselves to him, and when they found that everything possible was done for him as a member of the family, they detailed, day and night, three men to be ready for any emergency. Night after night I walked through the house and saw in the gloom those three dark forms and faces, motionless, only the eyes asking me if anything were wanted. They offered to detail a man to supply as far as possible his place as butler, this being a part of their system whereby to save one of their number from losing employment by sickness. At the same time a similar association of colored women, of which his wife was a member, detailed women to attend on and help the wife and care for the young children of the sick man, all of whom were members of the household. No wealthy white man in the land can, with all his money, command such unremitting devoted attention in his last illness as the colored men and women thus gave to one of their number. There was no moment in all the weeks of his sickness that there were not several men and women within call to supplement the attentions we gave him.

There have been sad mornings in that old house, when the daylight has come in on the dead faces of those of the family who have gone, but scarcely one more sad than that morning when his dark face was set, irresponsive for the first time.

His funeral was appointed for the third day after, and the daily papers gave notice of the hour at which would be buried, as the notice said, this "faithful steward and friend." His coffin stood in the very spot where had stood the coffin of the old father whose years of age and feebleness he had tended to their close; where had stood the coffin of the mother, whose saintly memory hallows the old house under the trees she loved; where each coffin of each of our dead in the old home had stood. He was a lover of flowers, and abundant bloom was around him. At the appointed hour the house began to fill. Every room, hall, staircase was crowded with an assembly of people, come there to honor a dead man worthy of all honor. His favorite hymn was sung with exquisite melody of voices. So, all the care and tenderness that we could bestow on our dead fathers or brothers we bestowed on him, for he was one of us.

But in the crowded assembly which came to honor the dead there were only two white men and four white ladies. Nor was this matter of surprise. It is not a special characteristic, so far as I know, of any one part of the North, that the color line should be drawn thus sharply. It is thus drawn everywhere. I have attended many funerals of colored persons, and in most cases have been the only white person present.

Writing about colored people reminds me of an old couple, who were once well known to many readers of this, and who have for some years past been citizens of another country, where they are happily settled. For there is a better country than this of ours, howsoever we may boast of our institutions.

The Church of the Transfiguration in New York is widely known by a name given it long since— "The Little Church Around the Corner." This was never a properly descriptive name, for it is not a little church. It seats nearly a thousand people, and is generally full. But the low ceiling, the wandering shape of the floor, the quiet and warm tone of the decoration, the paintings hanging low on the walls, and the numerous memorial windows, many of which are to children of the parish, give it a more compact and home-like appearance than some other churches, and lead strangers to underestimate its size. The members of the Transfiguration parish, old and young, are warmly attached to their church, and it is unnecessary to add that they are still more warmly held in bonds of very tender affection and respect to the rector, who is their father and friend. The church was founded by him and has always been under his guidance. It is a working church, reaching in its charities and ministrations all classes and colors of people. The record of these works is not to be published here. It is kept in a book elsewhere. Not the least interesting and important part of the work is among the colored people of New York, many of whom are members of the parish.

Old members of the parish remember George and Elizabeth Wilson, who for a long period were door-keepers and pew-openers in the church. Wilson was a tall colored man with gray hair and beard, a wrinkled forehead over a pair of fine eyes, a stoop in his back, and sometimes a halt in his step. For he was a rheumatic old man, quite feeble, never fit for hard work, and therefore a pensioner on the charities of the church. He did a little work, with his wife, in and about the church, which is, on week-days as on Sundays, always open for any one who may seek a place of rest and prayer. Elizabeth was not much better in health and strength than Wilson, but she was more active, and regarded the church as her special possession and care, for which she was responsible to the rector and to God. Wilson had been a slave in his younger days. Elizabeth was born free. At almost any time of any day you would be sure to find the two, moving slowly about the church, dusting here, cleaning there, arranging this or that; or perhaps sitting, silent, as if at home. They knew every member of the parish by sight, and on Sundays, standing at the transept door, recognized instantly any stranger, and showed him or her to a seat. They were a loving couple, closely attached to one another; devout and humble in life and conversation, much loved by all the parish. They had become, I might almost say, a part of the church decoration, for their forms made a feature of no little beauty in the home-like church. Their faces always greeted incomers with a smile of welcome, and when first one and then the other was missed there was a vacancy to which it took long to become accustomed.

They grew old under the care and in the service of the Transfiguration parish. Elizabeth was the first to go. There were some very touching, very thrilling occurrences in the room where she lay dying. None was more so than what old Wilson said to her just before she died. The last blessing had been given, the passing soul committed "into thy hands, O Lord." The rector and Wilson were kneeling side by side. The old man, silently weeping, held his old wife's hand. She was restless, and moved her head uneasily. Still holding her hand in one of his, he reached out the other, gently passing it over her forehead as if he would smooth the wrinkles, and said, "Never mind, never mind, Bessie darling, you'll soon be washed all white." No one had ever before these days heard him call her any name but Elizabeth. No one had ever before heard from him any suggestion that he desired to be of any other color. His heart now spoke out its hidden emotions, of love and longing, when he let his old companion go before him to the land of rest from labor, and of rank and station according to the will of the Master and King, in whom he had perfect trust.

He did not wait long behind her. He was very lonesome. He wandered in a vacant way around the church. He sat a great deal in silent thought there and at home. No one knows how lonesome life can be to a poor, old, rheumatic colored man, whose only companion of forty years has died. But he looked into the other world now with new thoughts and new desires. Elizabeth was there, waiting for him, white of countenance and pure of soul. Poverty and lowliness in this world compel miserable surroundings and associations with vice and sin and shame. The joys of paradise are not so entrancing to the vision of those who in this world live among the delights of life and the external refinements of society. The poor and lowly in New York cannot keep clear of the abominable surroundings of poverty; and to those poor who are pure in heart, as were Wilson and Elizabeth, the sight of the beautiful country over yonder is full of joy and refreshment and hope, even before they enter it.

At least once a week, sometimes oftener, he came to see us, and to talk about Elizabeth. Many visitors have been in my library, many dear friends, who have gone away forever. None of them have left here more enduring memory than he. He was a child philosopher, a child theologian. He told us what he thought, not as beliefs, not as opinions, but as ideas that had come to him when he sat alone thinking of this and the other life, and commenting to himself on the words of revelation. Wonderfully clear, marvellously penetrating are the wisdom and comment which come sometimes from such simple, thoughtful minds. He never knew he was talking theology or any other ology. He only revealed, with the simplicity of a child, the workings of a mind which had one great foundation principle of thought and reason—faith in a Saviour of men.

Wilson was a sensible man, without any imagination. Therefore we noted as more interesting and remarkable an occurrence which he related one morning, in my library, to one of the ladies who had been with Elizabeth in her last hours.

"I saw Elizabeth last night," he said.

"You dreamed about her, did you?" said the lady.

"No, ma'am, it wasn't any dream. I was awake, and she was in the room, and I saw her as plain as I see you." Being questioned, he described the vision. He always spoke slowly, and with choice of his words.

"It was all dark in the room, and I was lying awake thinking about her, and saying to myself, 'She is happy and comfortable;' and I looked up and she was standing by the side of the bed, looking just like she used to look a good many years ago when she was well and strong."

"Was she dressed in white?"

"No, ma'am, she had a kind of a mouse-colored cloak on, something like what ladies wear when it rains."

"And you were awake?"

"Just as awake as I am now, ma'am, and I had my eyes wide open."

"Did she speak to you?"

"No, ma'am; you see I was surprised, for it was dark, and I couldn't see nothing else; but I could see her just as plain as if it was light; and she stood still, and just kind o' smiled; but she didn't speak; no, she didn't say anything. She was lighted up, somehow, so I could see her. I was going to speak to her, but before I could get myself straight to say anything, she wasn't there, and I didn't see her any more."

Wilson had told his vision to some one that morning who had tried to persuade him that it was his imagination—a pure delusion. Not so we. Why should he not believe he had seen her? What harm in believing that God had sent her to comfort him in his lonesome old age? Who dare affirm it was not so? We encouraged him to believe it. Soon after that he saw her, and knew whether his night vision had been delusion or reality.

Both he and she died in the faith. The rector was with them to the last. One after the other was brought into the church, laid before the altar where they had worshipped with us, carried thence to the church cemetery, and committed to the earth until the resurrection.

Often and often I see visions of them, almost as plainly as Wilson saw Elizabeth. I see them when

I go down the transept, standing at the door as in old time. I think many of us who worship in the Church of the Transfiguration will be glad when we see them in the eternal temple, whose door and door-keeper is their and our Lord.

When you are passing through Twenty-ninth Street, turn into the church-yard, which with its shadowy trees, its fountain, and flowers and birds, separates the church from the street. Enter the church. It is always open; many weary men and women rejoice to find it so. On the right-hand side of the transept door, and also on the right-hand side of the baptistery, observe, as you enter, a stained-glass window. Perhaps this is the only window in any church in the world which is a memorial of a colored person. It was placed where it is, because that is the door which for years the old man and old woman—Wilson and Elizabeth—used to attend. The painting in the window represents the baptism of the Ethiopian by St. Philip. This is the inscription: "IN MEMORY OF GEORGE B. and ELIZABETH WILSON, *sometime door-keepers in this house of the Lord*. Ps. lxxxiv. 10." The reference is to these words: "For a day in thy courts is better than a thousand. I had rather be a door-keeper in the house of my God than to dwell in the tents of wickedness." They are not door-keepers now. No servant or apostle, not Peter for all his keys in symbolic art, keeps that door. For the King is himself the door, and no Peter keeps Him. Content, humble, and faithful as door-keepers in the church here, they walk now with kings and priests in the peace that is unbroken, the safe citizenship which is beyond all revolutions.

XVII

EXAMPLE

It was after sunset one evening, a long time ago. The road was good, and I had only four miles to drive. My horses were tired, for I had come a long way since noon and the sun had been hot. There was a sharp turn of the road to the left. At this point a new stretch of road diverged from the old road and joined it again two miles beyond. This two miles of the old road was a very bad road, and some twelve years ago the new road was laid out, over better ground. The old road was definitely abandoned, and at each end of it a lot of brush was piled across it as a barrier, so that strangers should not mistake it. In the course of years the brush heaps had decayed and disappeared, but the entrances to the old road had grown up with golden-rod and aster, so that there was no semblance of a roadway. That two miles of the old road was always a favorite drive for me. It was all in the forest, and was all very nearly level. In fact it was a bad road, because it was so level that the water did not drain away from it, and teams cut it up, and there were mud holes, and occasional projecting tops of rocks and uncovered roots of trees.

My reason for preferring a buckboard to any other wagon for ordinary use in the country is that it will stand rough work over unbroken ground. You can turn into the open fields or forests, and drive over rocks and logs if you drive with care, and your horses are trustworthy for such work. Logging roads, used only in winter with sleds, present frequent temptations to one who wanders around the country seeking beauties of nature, and with a buckboard one can often drive for miles into the apparently impenetrable forests.

I was perfectly familiar with this old abandoned road, knew where its worst places were, could crowd my buckboard into the brush and avoid bad holes. For the most part it was a good trotting-road, and as it would save a considerable distance to my tired horses and myself I took it. You will understand that I drove straight on into it, for the new road turned short away on the left.

The forest arched over the entrance. I went on at an easy trot for half a mile, then drew out sharp to the right to avoid a bad hole, formerly mended with logs, and now presenting the ends of those logs to catch and twist and smash a wheel. Then I plunged the horses' breasts into the low brush on the left of the road, and thus avoided the end of a great tree-trunk which had fallen and lay halfway across the old track, on the right-hand side. The twilight outside the wood was almost darkness here, but both horses and driver knew the road, and we went on at a fast trot for thirty rods, when I heard a piercing scream, followed by a succession of intermingled screams and shouting. It all came from behind me. I pulled up and listened an instant; then turned the horses into the low bushes, jumped out, and lifted the hind axle of the buckboard to the right while the horses swung around to the left, and drove back.

In the gloom I found some people who had come to grief. They were a man and a woman, who had been driving one horse before a buckboard. They had plunged into the hole and broken one wheel, then pulling instantly on the off rein had wrecked a fore-wheel on the log, and were thrown unhurt into the bushes. Their horse was an old logger, accustomed to catastrophes, and had stopped for orders.

There was nothing to do for these people except to give them a lift. Their buckboard was left where it stood. Mine was single, but the woman sat by me on the seat, and the man sat on the back end of the board leading his horse. For the uninitiated it may be well to explain briefly that a buckboard is a wagon whose seat stands on a broad spring-board which extends from axle to axle. The structure is simple, the riding on rough roads is very much easier than that of any vehicle on steel springs, and if properly built of good stuff it will carry a very heavy load. I drove slowly now. The moon, the harvest-moon, two days or so after the full, had risen, but moonlight makes a wood road more difficult to drive than darkness. It creates shapes and shadows wholly unfamiliar. It makes dark-looking holes across the road with the shadows of bushes or tree-trunks.

You have probably been wondering what these people were doing in that wild wood road. I had been puzzling myself with the same question, but had not asked it; in fact, little had been said—nothing that was not absolutely necessary. For when I found them their first words to me had been somewhat short and gruff, and I had neither thought nor opportunity of measuring them. I had been smoking a cigar when the screams arrested me. It was still between my teeth as they loaded into my buckboard, and I threw it away as I took my seat.

The world is made up of all sorts of people. It wouldn't be the world it is but for this fact. As in physical nature the wisdom of the great Director has provided compensations and balances, low grades of animals to devour filth and be food for other grades, thus forever rounding the circle of life, so it may be that He has intended some kinds of men and women to fill places in the moral world in which they have their uses, though we cannot discover what those uses are. What these people whom I had picked up in the woods were made for, what purpose they serve in the economy of moral nature, I don't know, unless they were made as irritants, mustard-plasters, blisters. Certainly we need that class of people sometimes. They were of a queer sort. As I took my seat and started the horses, the woman spoke. Naturally one might have expected something in the way of thanks. Nothing of the sort was there. She spoke in a semi-patronizing, semi-didactic way, expressing her sorrow not unmingled with offence at my being one of the sinners who use tobacco.

She gave me a lecture on smoking and drinking, which I received in humility. It was plain that she supposed me to be a resident of the country in which she was on a "mission." She talked glibly, and her companion occasionally suggested approval from the axle behind us. There was no convenient place into which I could dump them again, without hurting them, strong as was the temptation to do it. They did not seem to belong to any society or anybody, but were adrift, living on the country through which they drifted. The amount of false history, false translation, false quotation, false doctrine, and trash which this woman gave me, as an unlettered rustic, while I from time to time made a suggestion by way of ignorant inquiry, and so started her on afresh, was positively astounding.

I dropped them gracefully at the first house, and never heard what became of them. But as I lit a fresh cigar and the horses resumed their usual speed, I pondered on a part of the lecture I had heard.

It appeared that these people did not know their road, and having heard me say whither I was going, followed me, relying on me as a guide. Thus my example, in taking the wood road instead of the public road, had led them to disaster. "You are responsible for your example," is a common generalization, and the anti-tobacco woman reiterated the phrase. It is a favorite phrase with many enthusiastic advocates of total abstinence and many preachers of "reforms."

There are few doctrines more thoughtlessly and carelessly taught, even by men of intelligence, than this doctrine of responsibility for example. By this dogma life is walled in to the narrowest limits, loaded down with the heaviest burdens of responsibility for the sins of others. Life is no such difficult labor. When I drove that road I was under no obligation to inquire or to think whether any other person was going to put on me the responsibility of showing him the road. I deny absolutely any and every charge that I, by my example, led that party to a smash-up. Life would not be worth living if in all that we do and do rightfully and rightly we are to be held responsible for others who, following our examples, undertake to do the same things and do them wrongfully and wrongly. The strong swimmer is not chargeable with the death of the man who, seeing how easily he swims and thinking to do it as well, plunges in and is drowned. The tight-rope walker is not responsible for the broken neck of the fool who follows his example. The skilled hunter is not to be accused of the death by wild beasts of the unskilled man who emulates his deeds. The cool man of iron nerve who climbs precipices, walks on dizzy edges, leaps over deep chasms, has nothing to do as guide of the weak brain and legs which follow him to their destruction. In each of these, and in a thousand like cases, it is essential to responsibility that the follower who has gone to grief establish on his part a claim on the leader he followed, a right to take his example and guidance, and that he then follow the example exactly.

The path of duty in this world is a narrow path, and sometimes a very difficult path. But it ought not to be made painfully laborious. If the upright man, doing that which is right, following as closely as he can the example of his Master, who was once man among men, is to be told that his right-doing becomes wrong-doing because others may misinterpret it, that his praying may be a sin because others may think he is praying to idols, that his teaching of truth may be a sin because others may follow his example and teach error, that his pure affections may be sins because others may plead his example for their impure affections, that his temperance may be a sin because others may imitate him in eating and drinking, but do them intemperately—if, in short, the doctrine is true that man is responsible not only that his life and conversation be right, but also that his right-doing shall not be used by others to justify their wrong-doing, then duty is too complex for our humanity.

Grant that we are responsible for example in ill-doing, ill-living. That we are responsible when others follow us in right-doing and go beyond us into wrong ways is untrue. There is no difficulty in drawing the line. But the subject is muddled by careless teaching, and so muddled that people of vagrant habits and minds, like those I picked up in the woods, distribute damning error in connection with it. The woman said in substance that she could teach Christ himself to set a better example in a land of wine-bibbers.

XVIII

THE SIGN OF THE CROSS

THE minister was a Presbyterian and a low-churchman. He was a very low churchman. The difference between a churchman and a very low churchman is that the latter has little respect for the special considerations which make his church a church. There are churchmen and low-churchmen in all churches. The day of the old high-church Presbyterians is mostly gone by, except in the Scotch churches. The book of government of the church is pretty much forgotten, very much avoided, mostly unknown to the laity, and when discovered by some inquisitive layman is often explained away. It is very high-church. The low-church Presbyterian minister, earnest, sincere, a hard-working and devout man, had warm affiliations with all the clergy in the town and neighborhood, excepting one. He "exchanged" with them, giving his own people to understand that there was nothing in Presbyterianism which made it worth their while or his while to maintain it as a superior organization. He did not preach this doctrine, but he practised it. Once in a while he rejoiced the hearts of the old deacons and elders by a rousing sermon, in which he set before the congregation the distinctive features of the grand old church sanctified by the blood of the martyrs of Scotland, in whose faith hosts had gone from the toils and the moils of this world to the rest and the immaculate robes of the other. In such sermons he struck hard blows at Baptists and Methodists, sounding blows aimed at doctrines; and harder blows at Episcopalians, mostly aimed at practices; for he was a learned theologian, and he knew that the Thirty-nine Articles were Calvinistic enough to burn holocausts of Servetuses. Like thousands of the clergy of all denominations when they preach denominational sermons, he made the fearful error of teaching "how these people differ from us," instead of teaching the grand truth of the ages, how marvellous is the identity of most denominations in the essential doctrines of Christianity.

Whatever he was in theology, he was a faithful pastor of his own people, and untiring in seeking out the poor, the distressed, the neglected, the sinning. You may think you know hard-working men. I tell you there are clergymen of various denominations all over the world whose daily and nightly unceasing labors surpass all you ever imagined of hard work, and with constant surroundings of distress, misery, anguish. This clergyman lived a life of such labor.

There was an Episcopal church in the large manufacturing town, founded with express reference to certain families of English working-men. A rector who was called a high-churchman had been over it for some years. No one knew exactly what "high-church" meant, but most people had a tolerably correct idea when they said, with much indignation, "he thinks his church a great deal better than ours." Probably that was what he thought. That is what every Presbyterian, Methodist, Baptist, Lutheran, ought to think and teach of his own church. If he does not he has no business in his church. Other people thought him a high-churchman because the worship of God in his church was very ornate. There was no denying it. He had candles on the communion-table, which he called the altar; and he wore a stole with crosses embroidered on it: and he emphasized the *is* when he read "this *is* my body," uttering the words very slowly. There is no end to the things they said this high-church ritualist did, even to praying for the dead. But the most serious charge made against him, in the mouths of Christians of various names, was that when he gave the benediction he held out two fingers and made over the heads of his kneeling congregation the sign of the cross. I don't think there was anything in those days which many good people were so afraid of as the sign of the cross. Precisely what injury they feared was not definable, but no one ever feared the evil eye in the days of witchcraft with more sincere apprehension. Nor would this sketch be complete without the statement that the Presbyterian minister, while not foolishly afraid of it, did regard the use of this sign as a superstitious abomination, and talked and taught and preached as he thought about it.

Thus much as to what "they said" about the rector. Now as to what he was. No two men were ever more alike in spirit and life than the minister and the rector. The latter was a man of deep study, much learning, devout piety, complete self-abnegation, and devotion to the work of his ministry. He had been married, but his wife and two children had died—not gone away—for he had never considered his family broken up, had never stopped saying " give *us* our daily bread," precisely as when they knelt with him. This man was imbued with love for his Master and love for his fellow-man. His whole life was given to the work. He was day and night among the people, with those who were in trouble, with criminals in prison, and criminals who had come to him with confessions of sin and penitence, with the sick, the dead, the desolate. His ritualism, as it was called, was in his opinion useful in the work of his Master, and the crowded little church, the full Sunday-school, the working character of his young people in their little societies, the constant accessions to his parish—these attested some wisdom in his views. It began to be said that the poor people of this small church did as much charitable and reforming work as the richest congregation in the town.

It is not to be denied that there was some weakness, some foolishness in his ritualistic practices. No man is perfect in judgment. But his mistakes did no harm. Nothing that he did was aggressive. Ritualism has never been aggressive. It is always inside of churches, generally waging a defensive war against attacks of outside foes, and not often getting much sympathy from bishops. Withal this good man had, from long habit of study and lonesome devotion to his work, gotten the idea in his mind that other denominations of Christians were poor workers in the field of the world, other so-called churches very doubtful gates by which to enter the kingdom of heaven. He had adopted that very stupid custom of some churchmen, of trying to defy the law of language in America, and insist that it was wrong to use the word "church" except when speaking of his church. The preface of his own prayer-book, the statutes of his State, the literature of his age, the common-sense and common practice of the people which settles words—all were against him. But he lived in a world of his own, and rarely thought of any other—a common error, which injures many a good man's influence.

I have taken so much space in describing these two men that I have little left for my story.

There was small-pox in the town one winter, and wide-spread terror. Those are times when the people who are fond of abusing churches and clergy fly to them for aid. It is a queer characteristic of men who despise religion that they want the church near them when they or their dear ones are dying, and especially desire religious services at their burials. And it may be added that such men seem then to think the church an institution specially created for all men, though they never attended its services or paid towards its support. Now they ask its services gratuitously, accept them without thanks, and without repayment by any offering to church or minister.

The rector and the minister were everywhere among the poor victims of the pestilence. They had never met. One night the minister was told by the doctor that a poor Scotch woman, whom he had missed from her usual seat in the gallery of his church, was dying. He went through the snowstorm, wading in drifts and battling the wind, to a little lonesome wooden house on the outskirts of the town. It was midnight and after. No one answered his knock. He opened the unlocked door, entered a room, and saw, by a dim candlelight, a woman's form lying on a miserable pallet, and the rector kneeling by it, praying aloud for the soul that had just gone.

"Is she gone?" he said as the voice ceased, and he saw the rector make with his finger on the forehead, foul with disease, the sign of salvation.

"She is at perfect rest."

"Do *you* say that?"

"Yes, I have seen her often, before she became delirious. She was full of faith."

"You have been here often? and I have not! She was one of my people, not yours. I never knew she was ill."

"Yes, I know it. It was by accident I heard of her, and perhaps I ought to have sent you word; but I have been very busy. She was a simple, good soul. She loved the Master. He loved her. No pestilence comes where she is now!"

It was thus these two met. And it happened within the week that a very similar occurrence took place, this time the rector finding the minister with a dying girl, one of the children of the Episcopal Sunday-school. That day they walked away together, and fell into a conversation about baptism and regeneration, and each found that the other had thorough knowledge of what the Fathers and more modern theologians had said about it, and that they were not far apart in their own opinions. For they understood a fundamental rule that when men settle the meaning of common words in the language, they find that much apparent theological disagreement ceases.

They had thought themselves very far apart, and they found themselves very close together. When love lights the pages of controversial theology, it is astonishing how divergences vanish. There was not a bit of rancor, nothing but love in the hearts and lives of these two honest servants of the same Master. They parted that night, each surprised and very thoughtful; each convinced that between the Episcopalian baptismal " regeneration " and the Presbyterian baptismal "ingrafting into Christ" there was no difference which could be made clear to the poor mother of the dying child.

They met often after this, and each learned more. The minister discovered that in all human worship there is, of course, more or less ritualism, since "worship in spirit" means worship in person and purse, and men bend their knees in bodily ritualism when they desire to bow their souls in the humility of prayer. The rector learned that ritualism was good only when and so far as it would do good in the work he had at heart, and that the idea of substituting color symbolisms of church device for the settled color symbolisms of Europe, America, or China, was a vain imagination of churchmen uneducated in the various symbolic languages of the world.

I think the point on which they talked most was

the subject of Holy Orders. The Presbyterian learned to think more than ever of his church's teachings that his own ordination was in unbroken succession from the Apostles, through the laying on of the hands of the Presbytery. The Episcopalian began to consider, as he never had before, the fact that in his church a bishop, or a dozen bishops, cannot ordain a priest without the same laying on of the hands of the Presbytery. Time would fail me to enumerate the points of dogma or doctrine on which, in their now constant intercourse, they talked, opening their souls to one another.

Then grew up between these two men a mutual admiration and affection, which became warmer from year to year. They were men of God. In their humanity were weaknesses, imperfections, which their intercourse helped to show them. One in their faith, one in their purposes of life, in their object in work, in their devotion to one divine Master and His work in the world, they found infinite joy in helping each the other. Neither of them ever thought that his church was less fitted for the great work than the other. Each loved his own church the more, and while the rector became more wise in his ritual, the minister became more of a high-church Presbyterian. While the rector wanted to introduce incense, but never did, the minister allowed his young people to introduce, what is the same thing, odorous flowers to accompany and ornament worship.

· Time passed on, and those two men loved one another to the end. The rector went first. His life of labor wore him out at last. Besides, there were voices always calling him, and that almost always hastens the day of going. Too ill to stand or walk, he was carried to his native village in the up-country—to gain strength, said the doctor; to die, said the worn laboring man. Thither a few weeks later he summoned his closest friend, the Presbyterian minister, and for two days they held holy communion.

In the afternoon, just before sunset of the second day, there was a sharp, sudden change in the sick man. The minister had promised him, and now to fulfil his promise knelt by his side, opened the ready prayer-book, and began the words: "Oh, Almighty God, with whom do live the spirits of just men made perfect after they are delivered from their earthly prisons"—and there a choking sob interrupted his tremulous voice. For an instant he closed his eyes. Opening them he saw the face of his friend as the face of the first martyr, as the face of an angel, and knew that he was dead. And then the Presbyterian voice rose clear as he went on with the prayer: "We humbly commend the soul of this Thy servant, our dear brother, into Thy hands as into the hands of a faithful

Creator and most merciful Saviour. Wash it, we pray Thee, in the blood of that immaculate Lamb that was slain "—and so on till he finished the prayer. Though I know nothing about it, I have no doubt he prayed with and for his brother ever after, till they two met again and began together prayers that will be offered as long as souls exist and need anything from God.

The day his friend arrived the rector had said, "Will you read the prayer in the visitation service when I am dying; and will you read the committal in our burial-service when you bury me?" and the minister had said, "I will." So on a sunny afternoon, when all the people of all the country around were gathered in the village graveyard, the minister with clear voice said the words "earth to earth, ashes to ashes, dust to dust," sprinkling the mould on the coffin with his own hand.

Heaven was open overhead that afternoon. The angels saw the burial. The happy ones in paradise saw it all. The joyous soul, that had gone from the clay which was in the coffin down there in the open grave, saw on the coffin the dust his brother's hand had sprinkled in the form of the cross of the Lord, whom those two men had served as well as they could.

XIX

A CHILD'S VOICE

WE don't know half the time who are our fellow-travellers in this journey of life. I rode some hundred miles, and not happening to look into another car on the train did not see its occupants. When we reached the station, while some passengers were transferred to trains going on in one and another direction, and some were rushing for carriages and 'busses to hotels, I collided with a lady, apologized for the accident, looked just an instant at her face, and did not see her again. Riding up in the omnibus, I was conscious of a queer muddle of thoughts, caused by a glance at that face, in the crowd at the station. I had seen the face of a living, active, wide-awake person, but I had in mind the well-remembered countenance of one I knew was long dead.

When we were comfortably settled, and had washed off the accumulated dirt of various States, through which we had been dragged in what we moderns regard as the perfect style of luxurious travel, I sat on the piazza of the hotel looking at the mountains with no small delight. But I could not expel that face from my mind. As twilight came on there came with a click—a snap—a sudden flash-light on memory, which you have doubtless often experienced, the explanation, a very simple one, of my muddle. This face was probably that of a daughter grown to close resemblance of her mother who lived long ago.

It is very certain that the modern theories which ascribe memory to the arrangement of particles of the brain are based on insufficient observation of that mental action which is called memory. When asked if you remember an occurrence, and you reply "Yes," it may not and does not strike you what an innumerable variety of facts impressed on your mind are at once recalled to view. The occurrence is one fact, but the surroundings are hundreds, which go to make up the memory. Do you remember a face, seen long ago? You do, but what a complicated picture is that which, suddenly entering into your mental view, leads you to say "Yes, I remember it." The when, the where, a room, its furniture, its light, dress, ornaments, countless surroundings, external and internal, mental, moral circumstances, all go to make this instantaneous picture. If each of the almost infinitesimal particles of the brain received a photographic picture, with added colors, it would scarcely be sufficient to convey all the distinct thoughts and facts which come in the lightning-flash of a memory of one face, one landscape, one event.

But let us leave the mystery of memory to the vagaries of biology, while we rejoice in it as a possession which will be ours when the particles of our brains have ceased to ache with physical labors.

Into the soft twilight came the picture of a country church in a northern winter's day. All the landscape around it was white, except where an occasional pine-tree lifted its dark foliage. There were not many pine-trees left. For it was a part of the country long cleared and settled, and rich farms stretched over the rolling land in all directions from the village. But there were three great pines, grand wide-spreading white-pines, which stood in the graveyard close to the church. The sounds of the wind through them were many toned. In summer, when the windows were open and the breezes were gentle, the voices were musical; in winter, when the north winds raged, they were thunderous and majestic.

It was a splendid winter day, with a brilliant sunshine, and a stiff breeze drifting the snow in sheets and mists of gold and iridescent light. Within the old church were none of the comforts and luxuries of modern churches. The interior was plain; a gallery ran across one end; the pulpit was at the other end, high up, a round pulpit with a round sounding-board hung above it. It was reached by a winding stairway on one side. On either side of the pulpit was a high window, covered with green blinds, one of which was partly raised to let in light on the minister's sermon desk. Through that window you could see the dark branches of one of the great pines, waving solemnly, swaying slowly to and fro; and constantly, through the darkness among the branches, went sheets of sparkling light as the snow flew by on the wind.

Some of the pews were of a kind which few modern Americans have seen. These were the pews in the middle part of the church, in front of the pulpit, and were family pews, square, with seats running all around them. They were shut off from other pews, not alone by the high partitions, but also by silk curtains, a foot or so deep, hanging from bars above the partition rails. Thus the occupants of the pew were invisible to all other persons on the floor of the church. The pulpit was so high that the minister could see those who were facing him, and occupants of the end gallery could see those who sat with their backs to the pulpit. Those pews, I have said, were family pews, and they were well filled. Somehow, in modern times, it would seem that family pews are not much needed. Perhaps families are not so large. Perhaps the custom of going to church all together is not so rigidly observed. It was a sight to see a father and mother with six, eight, or more children, and perhaps some servants, file into one of those pews, and file out of it when the service was over.

The precentor was missing. He had never been missing before. Sudden sickness, an upset into a snow-drift and a smashed-up cutter, or some other unforeseen cause, had kept him away. There were plenty of men and women, any one of whom could have supplied his place if accustomed to stand up and sing in front of gazing people. But even in a country congregation, where everybody knew everybody else, that embarrassment which keeps so many good speakers and good singers unknown made it difficult to supply the place of the absent precentor.

Elder James Douglas was growing to be an old man. He was nearly eighty, but neither his bodily nor his mental strength seemed in any way abated. He was a man of courage, as his early life, in perilous times, had amply testified. Nor in his later years had any one imagined that he could be affected with timidity by the presence of man, woman, or devil. It nevertheless gave him a certain shock, the like of which he had never experienced, when the minister gave out the hymn and no precentor appeared in front of the pulpit. The elder sat in a pew at the foot of the pulpit stair. From the remotest times within the memory of the people he had taken the minister's place when the latter was absent. He knew that all looked to him to supply any existing need. But it had never before happened to him to lead in singing. The tunes in which he had joined with clear and correct voice for fourscore years were as familiar to him as the words of the oldest hymns. But every one who has tried it knows that for public speaking or public singing one must have a certain something back of knowledge of words or tunes.

The tall form of the old man, as he rose in the elder's pew and stepped out to the pulpit front, was the embodiment of courage, but there was no courage there. Still he started well, and the people, not knowing how weak was the leadership, joined heartily. The volume of praise was so full and strong that by the time they had reached the end of the first stanza the elder had begun to think he had discovered his vocation, and went boldly at the second stanza with full voice.

There is an old French proverb which teaches that it is only the first step which is difficult. Like many other proverbs it is a falsehood, sometimes costly, as many a man knows who has tried to walk a narrow plank across a river or a chasm. The elder made the common mistake of those who find themselves in unaccustomed paths, after boldly essaying the first steps. He looked ahead.

If you find yourself unexpectedly on your feet making a speech, and you begin to feel shaky, don't think ahead, don't look forward; just confine yourself to the work in hand, the sentence you are enunciating, and give no thought to what is to follow until you come to the end of what you are saying—in short, speak in public as you always speak in private conversation.

The elder began thinking whether he could carry the tune successfully over the notes in the next line, and, thinking, began to weaken as he sang. The voice which had been firm escaped his control, and only an uncertain sound murmured from his lips. Did you ever watch the process of the breaking down of a congregation of people who are apparently singing bravely together when the leader's voice falters? One and another voice follow him for a note or two; here one stops, there another, then a dozen, and a total collapse ensues. Thus it was now. All the people saw that James Douglas was scared, and the silence into which they fell was mingled with inquiring wonderment.

Whatever they thought was but for one instant. They were not singing, the elder was not singing, and yet through and above the strange rushing, throbbing sound of the wind in the pine branches there was another sound. Where did it come from? Was it a miracle? No one had ever heard such a sound in that church. The hymn was singing itself, in a child's voice, clear, sweet, the same tune, not loud, on the contrary quite low. The minister stood up in the pulpit and looked down into the pews. Elder Douglas swept his gray eyes from floor to gallery and gallery to floor. No one could tell where the sound came from, except only John Robson, who sat solitary in the front seat of the end gallery with twinkling eyes fixed on the minister's pew.

A child's voice, singing, is always melodious. To those who heard it then this voice was wonderfully sweet as it sang the words:

> "Other refuge have I none;
> Hangs my helpless soul on Thee:
> Leave, ah, leave me not alone."

The lost courage of the elder had now come back. He was not the man to think any sound supernatural which reached his physical sense of hearing. Others in describing the incident used to say that they did think for a while there was something uncanny about it. Not so the elder. He had been scared when he found himself trying what he had never before tried, the leadership of a singing congregation, and facing the awful idea that he might break down. Now the child's voice restored his confidence and faith in himself. His full, rich old voice joined the tiny treble, and then all the people came in together, so that the church was filled with their voices—

> "Still support and comfort me!"

and they finished the stanza in a fine burst of song.

Then came a trying moment. The elder and the people, and the minister too, as all afterwards confessed when they talked it over, having finished the stanza successfully, were one and all affected by similar thoughts. What had happened? What was that voice? Will I be able to lead this next stanza? Will the elder lead on? Will the voice be heard again?

Elder Douglas had no intention of pausing, but he did pause involuntarily, while he was wondering whether the child would again sing. A great gust of wind swept around the end of the church, and one of the long branches of the pine dashed its soft needles across the window-panes, and a deep sigh swelled into a sobbing voice, all in one instant; and then the little voice, all alone, was heard "Thou, O Christ—" It must be some child, said every one to himself or herself, and everybody, old and young, sang "—art all I want," and so the hymn went on to the end.

After the service the people talked, and asked one another who it was or what it was, but as no one could give any explanation they separated, with considerably more for Sunday-evening discussion than usual. But John Robson knew all about it, as he walked to the parsonage behind the minister and his granddaughter, who, with her mother, had come up for a winter visit. The mother was ill. The child had gone to church with the minister, and had been put alone into the great square pew, where she sat with her back to the pulpit and her feet on her grandmother's foot-stove, which John had placed for her before morning service began. John thought the front seat in the pew the proper one for children. So it was, according to custom, when older persons were present. John was always fond of telling the story, how he sat in the gallery and saw the eight-year-old child, shut out of sight in the great pew, singing her hymn right on, unconscious whether others were singing or not.

Where is the child now? Who can tell which way any one has travelled among the countless ways which led hither and thither from the door of that old church, ways in the world and ways out of the world? Was it her face, grown now to be like the face of her mother, which I saw in the crowd at the station?

XX

PURITAN SUNDAY

Do you know what that old and worn phrase, "A golden winter morning," means? If you have never seen it in our extreme northern country, of course you do not. It is not a poetic description, but plain English, describing the light. For the light makes the morning, and is the morning. Over all the country, far and near, rises from the snow a mist, invisible in the twilight and equally invisible after the sun is three hours high. When the sun comes above the horizon this mist is lit into yellow gold-dust. Around trees and other dark-colored objects there is a halo. Mountain-peaks seem to radiate light, and house-tops nearer to you blaze with lustre. If there has been a recent still fall of snow which has rested on branches of trees and leaves of evergreens, and this begins to drift lightly in the early day, it is more distinctly like gold-dust in the air. For nothing is white in this light, but everything partakes of the yellow tint, and the fields are covered with cloth-of-gold.

Yesterday morning was one of these golden mornings. And it was Sunday morning. And that made it more golden. For to you and me, my friend, who possess that priceless treasure of humanity, the love of Sunday, there is always an atmosphere on such a morning such as one may think they will enjoy who pass the gates of pearl. In summer or winter, in city or in country, Sunday morning brings to us great calm and peace.

They greatly mistake who imagine that in the minds and memories of all children who were brought up in the old-fashioned Puritan ways of "keeping" Sunday there is any pain or dislike to the day, produced by the rigidness with which we were made to keep it. You may find now and then one who likes to talk of the bigotry of that day in his childhood, but in the main it is not the Puritan children who when they grow old abuse the Puritan Sunday. With all its rigidness it was nevertheless a day apart from all other days, and it entered into the soul of the boy or the girl as another life, in another country, among other people, wholly other than the life of the six days. Perhaps in early manhood, in the whirl of active life and the absence of desire for mental rest, some may contemn the bonds of the old Sunday. But its memories are more deeply and more tenderly cherished by those children, now grown to be old men and women, than any memories of the other days.

One day in seven the boy lived more or less in company not of this world. He thought it hard sometimes, often. He had small love for the heroes of old Bible history, and a little more, but not very much, for Great-heart and Christian and the worthies of the allegory, wherein he read the story, but did not attempt to master the allegorical meaning.

But to-day, after fifty years in the work of the world, I challenge him, whoever he be, to answer you what part of his young life and young reading is most precious to him—what, if he must forget, would he desire now to retain longest? He will tell you that his memories of old Sundays at home, of Sunday mornings and Sunday evenings, of the church and its people, of family scenes, and books read with brothers and sisters and friends on Sundays are his most constant, most enduring, and most beloved subjects of memory.

I do not take any stock in the common saying of this day that the Puritan Sunday was injurious to the character of children, because they so gladly escaped from its bonds into freedom that they went to the other extreme. I believe if you could poll the honest vote to-day of the sons and daughters of old Presbyterian, Episcopalian, Congregational, and other families, in which they kept Sundays in the most rigid Puritan style, and who are now keeping it in the free-and-easy style of our time, they would be wellnigh unanimous in saying that they would prefer to have their children taught to keep Sunday as they used to keep it, rather than brought up as now, practically without any severance between the life of the first day and the life of the other six.

Not love Sunday because one was made to observe it too rigidly in youth! Don't believe it. No one that wasn't so brought up has a tenth part of an idea what it is to love it. What if it was hard on us? What if we do remember the longings we often had to be out of the bonds, the wish we often uttered that it were Monday morning! Now we know and feel that one day in seven, one month in seven, one year in every seven, we were out of this world, and in another world. For that is what Sunday then was. A world in which there is rest is another world than this in which we work. And whether we liked it or not, it made us know the reality that there is another world, just as plainly as if every Saturday night we had been sent to Asia, and made to pass one-seventh of our time there until we grew up and could go and spend our time where we pleased.

If a boy had been thus physically sent to spend a day in each week in some strange country, he would all his life remember most vividly what he saw there, and the people he met there, and this may be the reason why memories of old Sundays are more distinct as a rule than of other days.

How clearly the boy—for though he has lived to threescore and ten he is a boy still—how clearly he remembers the winter Sunday mornings, the ride to church, a sober sort of ride compared with that moonlight straw-ride on Friday night—with four horses and a jolly load in the sleigh—but a pleasant ride withal. He says nothing to the old folks as they turn the corner by the big chestnut-tree about what happened there. His mother remarks that the snow looks trampled as if a drove of cattle had been in the drift. He does not explain that as they went flying around that corner eighteen young people were hurled promiscuously into that drift, and the horses went tearing down the road with the upset sleigh, leaving robes and blankets all along the road till they brought up in the church-shed. No one is to know that fact, and it did not leak out till midsummer—too late to be a stopper on various other rides.

At the church door—he remembers now—there was some whispering with boys about that small affair. But in the church the thoughts of Friday night vanished, and the old man would not have remembered it at all but that he recalls that Sunday-morning ride and every little incident of it. For the old people he saw gathered there are now all gone, all now in that other country where they do not work and weary. They are to him now as people whom one has seen in distant travel, in peculiar costume, in a strange country.

Sunday dress is a feature in memory. People so dressed are wholly other than the same people in week-day dress. For why—they are indeed now of another race. That old brown coat, with its thick, high collar up to the very scalp of the head, is a queer, quaint old thing to remember, if you think of the coat only; but when you see it, the collar half hidden by the flowing white locks of the old man, who put it on every Sunday morning for fifty years as the ceremonial garment wherein he came into the presence of his Lord to worship Him, then it shines as bright as the embroidered chasuble of an Ambrose or a Gregory. That black poke-bonnet and black woollen shawl and black merino dress have no æsthetic characteristics whereby to commend themselves to recollection or by reason of which one should specially recall the thin, pale face of the old maiden sister of the farmer, whom you might have seen on Saturday in other dress doing her dairy work as she had done it close on to three-quarters of a century. But worn as they were only on Sundays, and only when she came to sit with her of Bethany at the feet of the Master, the black bonnet of the dear old woman is in memory bright with starry lights, and her shawl and dress are pure and shining as the white robes they of Sardis wear, walking now with Him where it is always a golden Sunday.

My pen has wandered away from what I began to write. The memories of the group in the church on the old-fashioned Puritan Sunday morning crowd in on me. They are gone into the country wherein they lived much of their lives here, especially the one-seventh of their lives called Sundays —the country wherein they tried on that day to make us learn to live also. Perhaps they did not succeed in bringing into this lower world the exact atmosphere of that to which they have since gone. But they impressed on our souls the ineffaceable truth that there is, parallel with this life, another wherein the patriarchs and prophets, the apostles and martyrs, the saints of many ages, the beautiful, the beloved, the holy women and stainless children are living while we are living here. When we remember them, the teachers of our youth, especially when we remember them on a Sunday morning in church or a Sunday evening by the fireside, we have no doubt at all that they are now in the pleasant country of their old hope and faith, with that admirable company whose lives they taught us to study on Sundays and imitate on week-days.

They were, many of them, very poor and very hard-working people. The ten-hour working-man of the city leads a life of ease compared with those up-country farming families. Before daybreak began and after dark ended each day's toil and labor of man and woman, and children so soon as they were old enough to work. And the reward was scanty—a bare subsistence, yielded by the hard soil which gave them nothing willingly, only graves when the work at last was over. No class of laborers on earth work so hard, and therefore need and enjoy the Sunday rest so much, as the farming population of our country.

And they loved the day, just as they kept it, or tried to keep it, in close conversation with another and better country. They loved the church and the service. There were stern and solemn countenances set on the face of the minister then. There were faces of exceeding human loveliness in the congregation. I wonder sometimes whether they get together now, whether in the time surely to come we shall all, or many of us, get together and send ringing out over the eternal hills the songs we sang here of a Sunday morning in the old church.

They will need no translation into that country's language. For that at least we learned in the Puritan Sunday, the language of the other world, and we can't forget it. It clings like mother-tongue, and it is the language of the mother of us all. So that if, perchance, where she now is, that dear old woman, whose lot here was poverty, and sometimes positive want, shall meet Martha or Mary, Elizabeth of Hungary or Brigitta or Lucia or Catharine, she will have no trouble in talking with them. Nor, if the Bishop of Ephesus should chance to walk by and speak with them, would he fail to understand her when she said in his own and her own language, "We do not hunger, neither thirst any more."

Yes, they talk one language there—a language you and I heard, if we did not learn, used, if we did not understand, in those old Sunday evenings; and depend upon it, however much we have forgotten the lessons of those days, there remains much of the good they did in others. And to-day the most powerful element for good in our country, the most conservative principle in the rush of social and political life around us, is that which yet remains to us of the old-fashioned Puritan Sunday.

THE END

www.ingramcontent.com/pod-product-compliance
Lightning Source LLC
Chambersburg PA
CBHW020822230426
43666CB00007B/1070